THE
TECHNIQUES OF
Traditional
WOODFINISHING

•

*To my wife, Monica – now I can relax, once
more, and finish all her urgent jobs*

THE
TECHNIQUES OF
Traditional
WOODFINISHING

BRIAN BARON

B. T. Batsford

LONDON

ISBN 0 7134 5165 3

Typeset by Latimer Trend & Company Ltd, Plymouth
and printed in Great Britain by
Anchor Brendon Ltd
Tiptree, Essex
for the publishers
B. T. Batsford Ltd.
4 Fitzhardinge Street
London W1H 0AH

CONTENTS

Acknowledgements

During the writing of this book I have been greatly helped and encouraged by many people and I am very grateful to all concerned. I thank especially Mr J W Collier, who took great pains with his teachings of traditional finishing in my early years of study, and also to Sonya Ernest who undertook the formidable task of typing the manuscript. I also thank Christine Jones, I.S.I.A.D. (1972–9), who provided the most excellent illustrations and Angela Blake for the time taken in producing the photographs. Finally, my thanks must also go to Mr E P Hudson who helped with the text.

Introduction

This book is intended to help anyone who is interested in the craft of woodfinishing. It should be useful not only to woodfinishers but to painters and decorators, carpenters and joiners, cabinet makers, upholsterers, modelmakers and anyone who is really interested in protecting the surface of wood. I intended it to be practical rather than designed for someone wishing to become a specialist French polisher, sprayer or woodfinishing craftsman. These crafts are only taught in certain areas of specific trades and take years of experience and knowledge. You can, however, learn skills and techniques that will improve the finish of your wood, learn how to use brushes, and apply surface coatings and colour. In addition, you can select your own textured coatings for a specific purpose and repair damaged polished surfaces. With your acquired skills and knowledge you will find woodfinishing both worthwhile and extremely satisfying.

CHAPTER ONE

History of shellac, materials, brushes

•

Shellac

The practice of using protective surface coatings goes back to Egyptian times. Various resins, oils and waxes were probably used for specific purposes, and therefore the protective coatings would have been oil-based materials. The Greeks, Phoenicians, Italians, Dutch, French and eventually the English all used oil-based materials to make protective coatings of some form or another. Not until the eighteenth century did resins become popularly used on a commercial basis, and the brothers Martin became famous for their production of varnish in France.

Oil-based resins, however, were slow drying, causing a problem with contamination, and it became obvious that some quicker drying material was required to speed up the drying of a surface coating. Thus the development and use of shellac based coatings became a prominent feature in the mid-nineteenth century. Shellac, is the commercial product of lac, the resinous incrustation from the lac insect, which forms the basis of varnish.

Shellac was by no means a new material. It was used around AD 250, even earlier as a resin varnish on an Indian imperial palace in AD 1590. Yet it was not until the sixteenth century that Jan Huyghen Van Linschoten in 1596 published his findings describing the lac insect and its product. In 1710 P Tachard defined the production of lac in an article, which was later followed by further publications of scientific descriptions given by J

Kerr (1781), W Roxburgh (1790), *Lac Cultivation* by B Hamilton (1800), and finally the *Anatomy of the Insect* by Carter (1861) and *Production of Lac* by O'Connor (1875).

The lac insect

The lac insect breeds on trees of the *Ficus* family in the East Indies. It is about 0.6–1.3 mm ($\frac{1}{40} - \frac{1}{20}$ in) long and in its larval form attaches to the bark of the tree. When settled it thrusts its proboscis into the bark and excretes a resinous substance over its body. The female becomes static, and at the end of eight or ten weeks the male emerges from its resinous coat and fertilizes her. The female develops into an amorphous organism, mainly comprising an ovary, from which the new larvae emerge. During the period of development the bulk of lac is formed and gathered on twigs.

Lac cultivation

This is a fairly simple process. The trees are pruned in season and infected by sticks of brood-lac. The larvae then swarm over the tree, thus settling on the shoots and producing resin. The crop is cut when ready; some is kept for more broodlac for the root crop, and the remainder is scraped off the twigs and sold. This scraping is known as 'sticklac', which is usually sold in the village markets to the manufacturers. Obviously there are varying qualities of sticklac depending on the broodlac and host tree, climate, harvesting, and methods of drying and storing it.

9

Lac conversion and shellac manufacture

The sticklac is crushed and purified by repeated washing in large vats of water until most of the impurities are removed. The lac is then spread out on a clean floor, left to dry out and then sieved to produce a seedlac. After the process is completed two types of shellac are produced: hand made shellac and machine made shellac. The seedlac is put into a long narrow cloth bag, one end of which is held in front of a charcoal oven and the opposite end is gradually turned. The heat of the oven melts the lac, which is then forced out of the cloth bag by pressure from turning the opposite end. The impure material is left inside the bag, and the hot lac is then scraped out onto a smooth porcelain cylinder, which is filled with hot water. The molten lac is then removed from the cylinder and

pulled off as sheet about 0.3 cm ($\frac{1}{8}$ in) thick. The worker then stretches the lac, with great skill, with his hands, feet and mouth pulling the lac in all directions to produce a transparent sheet approximately 1.5×1.2 m (5×4 ft) long.

Alternatively, hand made shellac known as 'button lac' is produced by dropping hot lac onto flat metal sheets to form circular discs or buttons roughly 5–6 cm (2–3 in) in diameter and about 0.6 cm ($\frac{1}{4}$ in) thick.

Machine made shellac is made by two methods, the heat process and the solvent process. The method using heat is to use steam and squeeze the molten lac through a filtering system using hydraulic presses. The lac is then stretched into long continuous sheets and broken into pieces to form the machine made shellac. The method using solvent removes the insoluble impurities by using industrial alcohol; the lac is then filtered through a fine cloth and rolled and stretched by machines. With this process a very high grade of shellac (with less than 0.2% impurity) can be produced, thus providing various types of shellac including dewaxed and decolourised shellac.

Properties of shellac

Shellac is hard, tough and brittle. It is odourless in cold conditions but has a distinctive aroma when hot. The best grades are light yellow and the inferior grades are orange brown to a deep reddish colour. Usually, lac resin contains some wax. Shellac is insoluble in water, glycerol and hydrocarbon solvents but dissolves in alcohols and organic acids. However, when heated up to 150°C the resin becomes more viscous and is polymerised. It is thus insoluble in standard solvents.

Uses of shellac

Various forms of surface coatings formulated with lac resins are produced, varying in colour, which are suitable for the different stages of application – namely, wash coating, seal coating, top coating and finally spraying. Originally lac was used as a dye and it is reputed to go back as far as 1000 BC. As a red colouring it was replaced by cochineal in the 1850s and from then on became used in many manufacturing industries. In Victorian times shellac varnishes and polishes were used extensi-

FIG 1   *Life-cycle of the lac insect*

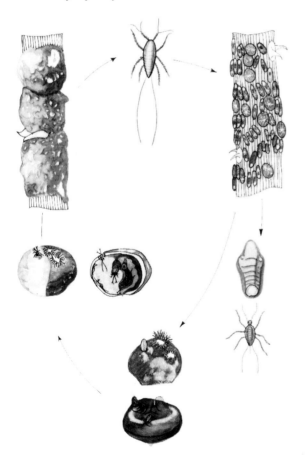

vely on furniture of all types, usually produced with a high gloss finish, and warm brown or mahogany in colour. Today, lac is a very versatile product, used in many industries such as printing, cosmetics, papermaking, ammunitions, footwear and, of course, woodfinishing.

Materials

The range of materials used by the woodfinisher is vast and extensive, helping you to produce various colours, transparent, pigmented and sometimes semi-pigmented.

Pigments

Pigments, either organic or inorganic, are solid particles incorporated into a medium but not soluble within it. A pigment provides colour and opacity, whilst at the same time it has the flow properties of a film. Pigments produce solid colours which can be used for blinding out unwanted colours or marks in timber. The development of pigments over the years has enabled the woodfinisher to use both traditional earth colours and synthetic pigments. Earth colours are usually umbers, ochres and other mineral colours. They are refined after being dug from the earth and then mixed into oil or water ready for use. The colours can also be burned or roasted (calcined) to obtain a change in their colour. Raw umber, for example, is grey in colour but when heated becomes a deep brown or, rather, burnt umber. Similarly, raw sienna (a yellow) becomes a reddish colour, called burnt sienna.

Raw sienna – This is brownish yellow in colour and made from iron oxide. It is mostly found in Italy and has great tinting strength, ideal for mixing into stains, graining colours and tinting whites. Siennas are good, lasting colours and have been used for many years.

Burnt sienna – After roasting raw sienna the colour changes to brownish red. This colour is then ideal for tinting where reds and pinks are required.

Raw umber – is another colour derived from Italy from the Umbrian region. It is very dull and is sometimes called Turkey umber owing to its common use in that country. Raw umber has good

tinting strength, is transparent and mixes well with whites. It is also good for mixing greens and cold colours which are fairly light fast.

Burnt umber – Again a colour which is roasted to produce a deep brown from greenish brown. Good for use in mixing stains and for graining colours.

Vandyke brown – A colour derived from the Dutch artist of the same name. A very valuable colour used to produce a whole range of browns. Excellent for stains and tinting and can also produce strong antique colours.

Orange chrome – A pigment with good tinting strength derived from the lead chromates, but tends to darken under acidic conditions.

Yellow ochre – Found throughout various countries, this is extracted from the earth. There is a whole range of yellow ochres, some of which are muddy. The pigment needs to be processed carefully to eliminate the coarse earth material if a good colour and strength of tint is to be produced. The ochre is ideal for yellow tints, pale creams, buff colours and some greens.

Many more modern colours are produced by chemical means and some of these are very strong in colour and expensive to produce. One of these colours is chrome, which is chemically produced by mixing, precipitating, filtering and squeezing.

Yellow chrome – A very bright yellow that is not good in light and usually darkens in colour. Other chrome colours are lemon and orange, which are also very bright.

Blacks – There are numerous black pigments that again produce various shades of black. These blacks can be produced by burning, grinding and blending.

Lamp black – This is produced by burning oil, resin or tallow slowly. It is a poor quality black and can be acidic if the burning process is not controlled. A good quality lamp black needs to have good drying properties and be of suitable tinting strength.

Drop black – A mixture of animal and vegetable blacks that are finely ground in water or oil. The best quality drop black is made by burning animal bones, then grinding them in water and later in oil, water and glue size for binding. The name drop black derives from the way it was sold, in lumps or drops. High quality drop blacks give really good colours and greys, olive, bronze, greens are sometimes mixed with them to produce special tints and shades in a white base.

Ivory black – Made from very hard bones by the charcoal-burning method and is sometimes called ivory drop black.

Black oxide – Synthetic black which is of small particle size; some iron oxides, however, are blackish brown in colour.

Blues

Ultramarine blue – Produced by burning. A combination of alumina, sulphur, soda and silica.

Cobalt blue – A very fine pigment giving good colour, strong in tinting strength, which has a strong resistance to sunlight.

Prussian blue – Sometimes known as Berlin or China blue and was discovered in Germany by a colour matcher. When the potash is mixed with iron sulphate a fine white pigment is precipitated and when exposed to the air oxidizes to a blue.

Greens

Chrome green – By mixing blue and yellow together we produce a chrome green which is highly resistant to sunlight and chemical attack. Very bright colours, clear and with good tinting strength.

Brunswick green – Not a strong colour but is used for tinting whites. A mixture of chrome lead and Prussian blue.

Reds

Probably one of the most popular colours in the pigment range producing quite a variety of reds. In the range there are vermilions, magenta (mauve), scarlet, crimson, rose pink. Some of these colours are lakes to which the woodfinisher today is not always accustomed. The lakes derive from coal tar bases but are now more complex and are manufactured synthetically from organic materials.

Vermilion – A strong, stable colour which is sulphide of mercury. The English and French vermilion tends to darken on exposure to air.

American vermilion is very bright but an expensive colour to produce. It is now replaced with other reds.

Magenta – A strong purple red. Tends to fade in sunlight and is really only a temporary colour. Derives from a coal tar base.

Scarlet – A sulphide vermilion that is more red than a true vermilion of the English or French product.

Scarlet lake – A natural lake deriving from madder (a herbaceous plant).

Crimson madder – Not very stable when mixed with other colours; tends to be clear. Made from the root of the plant.

Rose pink – Produced by using amaranth and acid rubine; it has good colour and tinting strength and can be used for tinting mahogany woodfillers.

Venetian red – A good colour for tinting some mahogany tones. Has good strength of colour, and is ideal for base stains and woodfillers.

Whites

Titanium dioxide

A very popular white used nowadays, giving excellent hiding power.

Flake white – An old white used very little today. Made from a metallic element which is bismuth.

Zinc white – A synthetic inorganic white made from metallic zinc at a high temperature. Very brilliant but not good under acid conditions.

White lead – Not good owing to its toxicity problems and, therefore, this limits its use in modern day surface coatings. Normally used in basic primers.

Extenders

These are base additives that help to modify a material. Extenders can be used in paste form for woodfillers and stoppers. Also, there are flexible putty-like materials which include putty, sealants and mastics. Some examples of extenders are as follows:

Barytes – Used in paints and woodfillers. An inorganic natural mineral, resistant to acid and alkalies.

China clay – A refined product used in primers and undercoats. Used for stoppers and wood-fillers and also matting agents in some pigmented coatings.

Gypsum – A base material used to produce plaster of Paris, which was commonly used as a woodfiller.

Silica – A very hard mineral which is good for making woodfillers. Sometimes coarse in texture but it can also be used as a matting agent in surface coatings.

Whiting – Composed of calcium carbonate and used in emulsions and water soluble paints. Acidic in nature and not good under these conditions.

Dyes

Dyes are similar to pigments but have slightly different characteristics. They need to have good solubility, be fast to light, resistant to chemical reactivity and finally have good shade and strength. Dyes are usually organic in origin, derived from animal and vegetable products and are not always stable under light. They can fade in certain conditions. However, they are ideal for tinting polishes, making spirit colours and general colour matching. They provide good clear translucent colours of varying strengths.

From the woodfinisher's viewpoint it would be wise to mix your own dye colours and strain some of them in order to produce good clear colours. Dyes can be mixed in oil, water and alcohols. When mixing dyes it is important to use enough dyestuff so as not to produce a saturated solution, otherwise the undissolved dye may bleed out into the surface coating being applied. The aniline colours are particularly suitable for mixing stains, the most common ones being reds and blacks. However, there are many other aniline colours too.

Whatever colours are used it is advisable to fix the colours with some sealing coat to make the dye colour stable. Usually some type of shellac base material is used.

Stains

Stains can be produced in certain categories, these being:

Type	Drying rate
Oil stains	Very slow
Water stains	Slow
Water pigmented stains	Slow
Chemical stains	Slow
Spirit stains	Medium fast
Mixed solvent stains	Fast
Non-grain raising stains	Very fast

Oil stains – Although very slow in drying, these stains tend to be quite popular owing to the ease with which they can be applied. They are usually based on naphtha or white spirit solvents. Bitumen based, they can be tinted by the oil soluble dyes. Oil stains tend to like hardwood timbers but are not usually suitable for softwoods owing to the content of bitumen. The bitumen tends to strike heavily into the imperfections in these timbers.

Water stains – These tend to be rather cheap and are good for producing an even colour. They do not penetrate well in the timber but are ideal for awkward timbers such as beech. Other stains such as oil stains tend to cause problems with beech timber owing to its lack of uniform grain structure.

Two of the most popular colours in this category are vandyke brown (powder or crystals) and mahogany red (powder or crystals). However, because of changes in manufacture the trend is now to supply these colours only in powder form. You will find that owing to lack of penetration, evenness of colour is difficult to obtain, and a certain amount of skill is required in applying these stains.

Water pigmented stains – With technological progress it is now possible to have stains which produce very bright colours. These rely on the use of microfine pigments that allow more colour to be introduced into timber initially. However, they do tend to obliterate the timber to a greater extent.

Chemical stains – Many problems can arise when you use these materials because they react with the acid content within certain timbers. Potash solutions, sulphates, liming agents, ammonia, acids, alkalis and salts also present such problems. However, the skilful woodfinisher can produce a range of good clear colours, depending on the particular type of timber being stained. Always mix these stains carefully and use a test piece of timber before staining the actual work.

The potash solution, one of which is bichromate of potash, can produce a whole range of colours on mahogany timbers. Sulphates produce much colder shades and can make timbers look much older if you carefully select and apply them.

Lime solutions are ideal for use on oak and pine timbers. Oak is darkened when you apply caustic soda, ammonia or lime. When treated carefully, oak lends itself to a beautiful range of colours; reproduced colours are normally acceptable on wall panelling, contract work and specially designed furniture.

When applying ammonia on oak timbers the colour changes to various pale shades of brown, but if the timber is 'fumed' you get a green colour known as 'fumed oak'. In this instance only the fumes of the ammonia are used. Soda on oak when Venetian red or brown umber is added produces an opaque stain.

When applying chemical stains remember that because of the nature of the timber, the grain will have risen; sometimes it is advisable to raise the grain initially by damping down the timber with water. Also note that some acids, notably nitric, may be used to age timbers.

Bleaches

One of the traditional ways of bleaching, especially on oak timbers, was to use alum (mineral salt), which used to be applied on shop fittings of good quality oak veneers. However, we now use more complex bleaching solutions which are very powerful. Another bleach, not quite so commonly used nowadays, is sodium hypochlorite which takes the red out of mahogany timbers. Readily available commercial bleaches can also be used, which are quite cheap but have only limited bleaching action. The most popular bleaches used today are the so-called two pack bleaches, which are based on one solution of caustic soda 'A' and the others of hydrogen peroxide 'B'.

You should apply the A solution first and allow this to penetrate into the timber. The bleaching action of the solution will bring out the red in the timber. When this has taken place, apply B solution on the A solution and you immediately see a change in colour. There should be a lightening action of the timber to a pale straw colour. Allow this lightening action to take place for about 15 minutes and then wash off all the bleach with plenty of cold water. It is essential to remove all the crystals that may occur so that no bleaching solution is left in the pores of the timber. A stiff scrubbing brush is useful for cleaning out the pores with water. Traditionally, oak, walnut, birds eye maple and some mahoganies were bleached, and when the timbers were carefully selected for good grain effect they proved to be very exotic in appearance.

It is worth mentioning that bleaching is now no longer popular because people prefer the colour of the timber. There is also the problem of washing and cleaning the timber which is very time consuming and therefore expensive. Finally, if the bleaching solution is not properly washed out of the pores of the timber, trouble could arise at a later date owing to bleaching agents reacting under the surface coating applied. However, if you work the stages very carefully as previously mentioned, no problems should arise.

A point worth noting is the effect of 'blistering' which can occur on some glued veneers which were applied on pre-war furniture. The two pack bleaches are usually the cause. They should be used with care.

Woodfillers

There are numerous types of woodfillers which help the woodfinisher to provide a nice smooth surface on timbers. Woodfillers can be grouped into three main areas: oil bound, resin bound and catalysed fillers. Each type has its own particular function. Normally woodfillers would be used on open grain timbers, and these materials help to save time as well as colour the timber.

The use of woodfillers will be dealt with later in the book, but the main ingredients are filling powder, extender, binder, colouring agent and solvent. By careful selection of these ingredients a woodfiller of good filling properties can be produced that will be stable under most surface coatings.

Dyes can also be incorporated in fillers to introduce added colour to the pigments, thus making the filler colder or warmer.

One of the better filling powders used in manufacturing woodfillers is silica – a fine powder which settles well in a medium. The extender is added to create a varied texture in the formulation and one such extender is China clay. Choose an extender very carefully in order not to cheapen the produce and sacrifice adhesion for good settling properties.

A binding agent (binder) is important in as much as it determines the characteristic of the woodfiller. One such binder is the oil-bound type which can have such materials as alkyd varnish, linseed oil, copal varnish or gold size added to the ingredients. However, these materials are relatively slow drying. We can also introduce a much quicker drying agent in relation to binders by using a resin-bound material which promotes a decrease in the drying time and therefore an increase in production.

The catalyst-type woodfillers are a little more complex and consist of a two pack system in which a polyester-type resin and styrene combination are mixed with an organic peroxide. In this system the styrene crosslinks with the resin and the surface coating. The problem with these fillers is that they dry quickly. The fillers have limited pot-life and therefore on large scale work really need two workers to use them – one to apply the filler and one to remove the surplus.

One of the oldest known woodfillers is plaster of Paris. This is a very good, hard filler but tends to show the whiteness through the surface coating. This problem can be overcome by adding a pigment colour. It is a somewhat messy filler to use but quite stable long term.

Special woodfillers can be mixed by introducing bright colours into a base filler, usually a light natural filler base. These colours can be green, blue, red or even metallic to provide a decorative effect with the grain structure of the selected timber. Some of the suitable timbers which can be filled with these special fillers are elm, oak and ash.

Traditionally, before woodfillers became popular, polishes were used to fill the grain pores of the wood. Obviously the open grain of timbers such as oak and ash necessitated a great deal of work so now manufactured woodfillers are used. There are simple recipes for making your own particular colour of filler and these will be dealt with later.

Rags

There is a whole range of types of rags made from natural and synthetic materials and it is advisable to select the right one for the particular work in question. When you apply woodfillers you should use an old coloured rag, preferably made of old wool or thick cotton material. Then remove the surplus woodfiller with hessian or old sacking made of flax or hemp. The weave of these materials helps to pick up the excess woodfiller from the surface of the wood and provides a clean wiped surface. Some woodfinishers like to apply woodfillers with hessian, but in my experience

FIG 2 *Types of rag: mutton cloth, hessian, coloured rag*

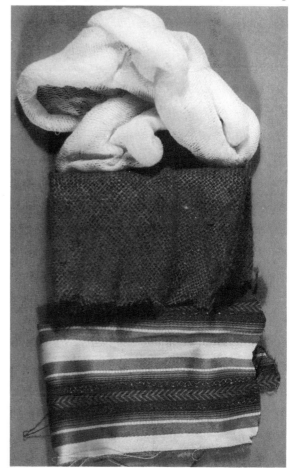

15

removing surplus woodfiller with hessian is much better.

When staining use old coloured rags for application and also for general dusting down from time to time.

It is essential for a woodfinisher to choose carefully the ideal rag for applying French polish. These rags are normally linen-type or heavy old cotton cloth which must be 'lint free'. The rags should have good 'bite' on the work surface to produce good results. The flow of polish through the rag is important, and therefore the correct texture of the material is essential. Polishers will sometimes use old 'worked in' *rubbers* with the cloth removed, known as a 'fad'. This fad helps the polish to flow more easily onto the timber surface. Special rubbers for piano finishings are used, and these are normally made up from heavy cotton cloth. This very tough surface helps to flatten the polish down, thus producing a really good polished surface for later finishing. At the final finishing stage, use a good quality chamois leather cloth or damask to spirit out the finish.

When applying stains you can use old rags,

FIG 3   *Types of rag: velvet, white rag, wadding*

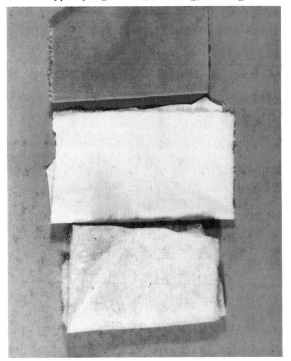

made of synthetic fibres, although they do not 'bite' on the surface. Wherever possible, therefore, use old coloured *cotton* rags for applying stains. Mutton cloth is ideal for applying soft polishing waxes and buffing up the waxed surface and is also good for applying polishing creams. Old stockings and tights are good for straining stains, some paints and varnishes.

At one time a polisher may have used a velvet with the rubber and would have applied a 'half and half' polish and varnish mixture, which would leave very few marks. The modern equivalent to this velvet is the paint pad, which can now be purchased in your local DIY shop.

Wadding is used for making the polisher's rubber, normally with its surface skin removed. For this do not use medicated cotton wool because it will clog up easily and cause problems. If you don't have wadding available use an old woollen sock which will give you a much harder rubber but at the same time will be quite flexible.

For dusting down your work use a 'tac rag'. This is a fine muslin, impregnated with a non-drying oil, which when used over the polished surface removes the dust. It is ideal for using between coats of polish or lacquer.

With experience you can achieve good results by selecting and using the correct rag for your particular work in hand. The rags are supplied to the polish and lacquer stockists; these are often old hospital bed sheets which are not always suitable for polishing rubbers, but best quality white polishing rag is difficult to obtain.

Abrasives
Selecting the correct abrasive material can be difficult when smoothing a timber surface, cutting back polish or burnishing a surface coating. Garnet paper is probably the most commonly used abrasive paper in the furniture trade and is graded by the size of the cutting grits. For example, the grit sizes are numbered 10–600 or have an '0' number which could be 1/0, 2/0, 3/0, etc. Abrasive papers which are called 'open coat' papers are coated with less grit. The paper backings can be of various flexibility depending on the paper grade. This paper may be waterproofed with resin, which also helps to stiffen it. There are also linen-

backed abrasive papers which are usually emery cloth abrasives. They have carborundum and magnetic abrasive particles on the linen surface and are usually used for preparing metal.

FIG 4 *Abrasive papers: lubrisil, garnet, silicon carbide, aluminium oxide, floor paper, steelwool*

Traditionally the polisher would have used glass paper coated with flint or a flour paper coated with glass. However, these papers have now been replaced by the garnet papers, which last much longer.

There are other alternatives to garnet papers, however. Lubrisil paper is coated with a fine 'talc' powder which helps to promote slip to the surface when sanding or de-ribbing. It provides a smooth papered surface on polish and lacquers. The silicon carbide type of abrasive paper can be used wet or dry and when used wet the wetting agent could be water, soap and water or a thin oil which could be white spirit (turpentine substitute). Fine grade wirewool (steelwool) can also be used for cutting back polished or lacquered surfaces and you should take care to abrade evenly with the grain. Use grade '0000' for fine abrading and grade '3'

for stripping off old polished or lacquered surfaces.

One of the oldest abrasives is pumice powder, which derives from volcanic rock, and can be used with a damp rag or fine dusting brush. It is also used in block form by decorators and for 'donkey stones' which are used to clean the front doorsteps of houses in north west England. A pigment is added, usually yellow ochre, to produce a cream stone that helps to colour the stone doorstep.

Abrasives can also be incorporated in waxes which can be hard or soft; these wax abrasives are used for cutting compounds and wax finishes on surface coatings. They help to cut back the polished surfaces to a flat smooth finish or a flat surface ready for the next stage in finishing.

Oils

The most popular oils used in polishing are linseed oil and white oil. Linseed oil is used for lubricating the polish when using a polishing rubber and for the manufacture of oil-based paints.

Most polishers prefer linseed oil rather than white oil for lubrication as white oil tends to be greasy and difficult to clear when final finishing.

There are numerous other types of oil which can help the woodfinisher, one being camphorated oil, which is used to remove mild heat or water marks from a polished surface. Red oil was made by using alkanet root to dye linseed oil and then applying the dyed oil on baywood, mahogany or walnut, which requires a warmer tone. Tung oil, which is fast drying and ideal for use in paints and varnishes, has good heat and water resistant properties. Soya bean oil is sometimes added to linseed oil to cheapen the product without loss of performance. It is good for grinding some pigment colours. In general most oils are used in the manufacture of paint and varnish products and have various degrees of drying properties. Some oils are classed as non-drying oils.

Waxes

Beeswax is commonly used in woodfinishing but it is blended with other waxes to provide a more easily manageable wax for application purposes. Sometimes a pigment colour can be added to promote a colour in the grain of the wood. Paraffin wax is used in some matt lacquers, finishes for floors and some furniture waxes. There is usually a blend of cellulose soap solutions in some waxes with added carnauba wax, which helps to provide hardness in the wax blend.

There are also emulsion-type waxes with added pigments for colour. These waxes are ideally suited for light timbers such as pine or oak and are used for one coat finishes on these timbers. Burnishing waxes have added abrasives to help the cutting action on surface coatings. Fine powders are mixed into emulsion-type waxes for wax pastes and creams. A dark pigment can be incorporated into the mix so there is no white deposit left when they are applied on open grain timbers.

Silicon waxes are very tough and are resistant to water. They are now used in modern waxes for furniture restoration and are sold in tins or aerosols. The problem with these waxes is the refinishing at a later stage. The wax needs to be completely removed so that adequate adhesion of the newly-applied surface coating is executed.

Solvents

These materials carry the solids and can be mixed with each other. They dissolve solids, thus creating a solution. These solvent mixtures are complex and formulated to modify the viscosity of a surface coating. A solvent must be effective, have the correct evaporation rate for a desired film and minimal toxicity, and be reasonably priced. A solvent for a particular resin may not be suitable for another resin so a diluent is added. Diluents are often cheaper than true solvents. The two most important factors concerning solvents are the solvent power to dissolve specific resins and the evaporation rate that is relative to the speed of drying.

Some common solvents used in surface coating manufacture are as follows: aliphatic hydrocarbons, such as white spirit; aromatic hydrocarbons, toluene and xylene; esters, ethyl acetate and butyl acetate; ketones, acetone and methyl isobutyl ketone (MIBK); glycol ethers, ethylene glycol monoethyl ether; and alcohols, ethyl alcohol, and butyl alcohol.

One of the most popular solvents used by the woodfinisher is ethyl alcohol which is a pure alcohol with added methyl violet (IMS). This is industrial methylated spirit and is normally used in French polishes, spirit soluble dyes and some synthetic resins.

The aliphatic hydrocarbons are used for oil paints; they dry slower and will dissolve most oils, natural resins, oleoresinous varnishes and alkyd resins. White spirit is very common in this group.

In the aromatic hydrocarbon group, toluene is used in some cellulose-based coats and acts as a diluent. Xylene is commonly used in polyurethane varnishes, some vinyls and alkyd resins. It is a slow solvent allowing flowing of the film.

Cellulose materials usually rely on the addition of ethyl acetate, which tends to tolerate the alphatic hydrocarbon diluents more easily than coatings with ketone solvents. The odour of these solvents is much more acceptable than cellulose coatings supplied by the retail market. Butyl acetate, however is used in paint formulations and is a solvent that dries moderately quickly.

In the ketone group, acetone, being a very powerful solvent with a fast evaporation rate, is used in vinyl and nitrocellulose formulations. It is used in small amounts to modify other solvents which may also help to modify the properties of a surface coating. Methyl isobutyl ketone has a moderate evaporation rate, being a solvent for polyurethane and cellulose surface coatings.

Some resins require a slower drying solvent, and therefore ethylene glycol monoethyl ether is frequently added to surface coatings which require brush application. One common brand in this group is 'Cellosolve'.

The alcohol groups provide the paint and lacquer industries with commercially available solvents for use in cellulose furniture lacquers and the methylated spirit used in shellac polishes. The butyl product is used in oil-type, acrylic-based and cellulose coatings.

One group of solvents not mentioned is the chlorinated type. These solvents are used in cleaning solutions and stripping solutions. One such solvent in this group is methylene chloride, which is commonly used in the manufacture of paint strippers.

When choosing a solvent try to select the correct one. Often the term 'thinner' is linked with solvent but remember that the thinner used may be a solvent mixture that reduces the viscosity of a solution.

Solvent thinner	Type of material to be thinned
Water	Water based emulsions
	Water soluble dyes
	Water pigmented stains
Esters	Polyurethanes (two-can)
Xylol	One-can polyurethanes
(IMS) Methylated spirits	Shellac polishes
	Shellac varnishes
	Shellac sealers
	Spirit soluble dyes
(MEK) Methyl ethyl ketone	Cellulose
(MIBK) Methyl iso-butyl ketone	Cellulose
White spirit	Oil stains
Naphtha or xylol	Naphtha stains
Proprietary thinner	Mixed solvent stains
	Non-grain-raising stains

It is worth the effort of obtaining the appropriate thinning solution. Try to adopt the practice of storing a small quantity of solvents which you use regularly. Solvents being complex materials do go 'off', so it is impossible to stock a complete range. Nowadays manufacturers produce what are known as 'dual thinners'. This solvent is designed to reduce the viscosity of standard cellulose materials and helps to save cost in solvent production and bulk storage. If you don't know which solvent to use always test the liquid with a small proportion of the selected solvent first. You may make some errors occasionally, but remember, practice makes perfect.

Cleaning solutions

These solutions may have methylene chloride incorporated in the mixture. They destroy solids which need to be removed. Wood may need a further washing in detergent to clean the surface thoroughly. Most workers tend to wash their hands with these solutions, which is inadvisable as they dry the oils in the skin. Always wash your hands in normal soap and water after using these cleaning solutions.

Matching colour

Designed for use with sprayguns, these colours are based on dyes and pigments dissolved in cellulose solvents, with a small amount of cellulose lacquer added to act as a binder. They are not suitable for hand application because of the fast rate of drying. Shellac-based colours are also produced, but the tendency is to use the quicker-drying cellulose colours which are normally designed for use in a complete finishing system.

Resins

For use in surface coatings, resins were of a natural origin up until the early twentieth century. They consisted of natural resin – very hard non-crystalline solids which are broken into pieces. They are insoluble in water and are sometimes completely or partially soluble in some of the organic solvents such as alcohols and hydrocarbons. They are heated to release a very sticky viscous fluid.

The terms 'gums' and 'resins' were often used synonymously but they are different. Gums are soluble in water but not in organic solvents; resins are insoluble in water and partially soluble in organic solvents.

Resins are now classified into various groups, these being:

Natural resins – This group, obtained from trees, produces a soft sticky resin. One such tree is the pine which produces oleoresin. The manila and damar resins are also soluble in alcohols and hydrocarbons and are sometimes used in the spirit varnishes. The fossil resins are dug up from the ground; they come from trees which have long since decayed. In this group we obtain the congo and kauri copal resins. They are normally used in oil-type varnishes and are soluble in some organic solvents. Finally there is the lac resin, mentioned previously.

Modified natural resins – These are the esterified group of gums and copal esters and the partially semi-synthetic types which are derivatives of resin, such as maleic resins and phenolic resins.

Synthetic resins – These are produced by the condensation or polymerization reactions from organic compounds, such as phenolic resin and coumarone resin.

Production and properties of resins

The trees that produce the resins are tapped under controlled conditions, and the resin is known as 'oleoresin'. When exposed to the atmosphere, evaporation, oxidation and polymerization may occur resulting in the formation of a solid; sometimes the proportion of oil essence turns this into a flowing liquid.

The copals, which are soft compared with fossil type resins, which are in the ground, can be heated too to make them soluble in oil. The damar resins are soluble in aromatic hydrocarbons but insoluble in alcohol.

Resins are graded for use in surface coatings for colour, gloss and adhesion. Some of the synthetic resins are very glossy and adhere well to timber. They are ideal for surface coatings in the furniture and allied industries.

More synthetic resins are used in the manufacture of surface coatings than ever before owing to modern paint technology. We now produce and use acrylic resins, polyester resins and polyurethane resins. These resins are very durable and hard and provide a finish with more gloss and better adhesion. We now have a situation where the formulation of film can be produced in almost any formulation with specific properties. The paint chemist can thus provide surface coatings of greater complexity.

French polish

A selection of shellac resins can produce a range of polishes of various colours, the 'lac' being dissolved in methylated spirits to produce the desired type of polish. Introduce other ingredients, such as gum benzoin to provide a bright effect or cellulose to increase the flow of the polish. If you require some element of heat resistance use natural resins incorporated with damar or another synthetic resin. A soluble dye is used to obtain a black or red polish. These dyes are nigrosine or bismark brown.

Traditionally polishes are produced in certain types: button polish, garnet polish, white polish, transparent, pale, french polish and orange polish. There are also ranges of shellac sealers which are ideal for sealing coats and generally include chalks or stearates. Because polish changes colour in metal containers, it is now supplied in plastic containers, usually in $1 \, l$ ($\frac{1}{2}$ pt) or $5 \, l$ ($7\frac{1}{2}$ pt) sizes. Shellac-based materials are ideal for use as sealers before further modern synthetic coatings are applied. French polish, however, is not heat resistant, is reversible and can suffer from contamination by water or alcohol. We class French polish as being thermoplastic.

If polish is applied correctly the appearance will be pleasing, and although it is somewhat vulnerable, it usually looks as good as any other surface coating. When buying polish you may obtain a price list from a polish supplier, individual suppliers usually stocking a range of those.

Varnishes

Varnishes come in two types – oil-based and spirit-based. Nowadays, however, there are upgraded oil-based types using urethane resins, which are highly resistant to certain conditions.

An oil varnish will usually contain linseed oil and possibly a natural resin, which could be a copal or damar. This will dry by oxidation and has trade names such as yacht varnish, church varnish, carriage varnish or even oil varnish. Oil varnishes have good elasticity and gloss and come in various colours – white, pale, medium or dark. Colours can also be added to obtain a desired colour tint.

Spirit varnishes may contain a kauri gum together with methylated spirit which dries by solvent evaporation. Coloured dyes may also be introduced into these varnishes.

The urethane resin varnishes are quite hard but just as resilient as the standard oil-based varnishes and tend to crack under certain conditions. They can be used both inside and outside and are suitable for the shop-fitting and building trades.

The performance and application of the various varnishes will be dealt with later in the book.

Stoppers

These materials are sometimes confused with fillers, woodfillers and grainfillers; the latter, however, are for grain filling only whereas stoppers are for filling splits, cracks and dents in timber. Stoppers are made of whiting, chalk and other extenders, which are formed to make up a paste, which can be either water soluble or a cellulose-type dissolved in cellulose solvents. The water soluble type usually incorporates a pigment to colour the wood, and the cellulose-type has a white or grey base colour that can be used on timber or metal. Other stoppers are made from hard materials, such as shellac stopping. This stopping is produced in various colours – from white to black – and is known in the finishing trade as sticklac. These stoppers are best suited under French polishes.

One other stopper which was well known up to the second world war was beaumontage. It was said to have been first produced by a person named Beaumont, over 80 years ago. A mixture of beeswax, crushed resin and pigment is melted in a tin to produce a coloured stopping. The colour can be changed by introducing any desired pig-ment colour. The stopping is used to fill any crack, split or dent in the timber and is then finely chiselled away. The surface is then papered down until smooth and is then ready for the next finishing stage. Beaumontage is thus very similar to our modern sticklac.

Plastic wood is now an old and trusted stopper which dries hard and is cellulose-based; it is ideal for stopping up chipboard surfaces. One other type of stopper is 'cellulose jam' which is cellulose lacquer allowed to dry semi-hard. With a pen knife, apply the semi-hard lacquer into the damaged area of the lacquered surface, allow to dry and then scrape off the surplus with a sharp razor blade. Sometimes raw beeswax is used for stopping up small dents and scratches in French polished surfaces. This is soft, however, and is not really suitable for anything larger.

FIG 5 *Various types of stoppers*

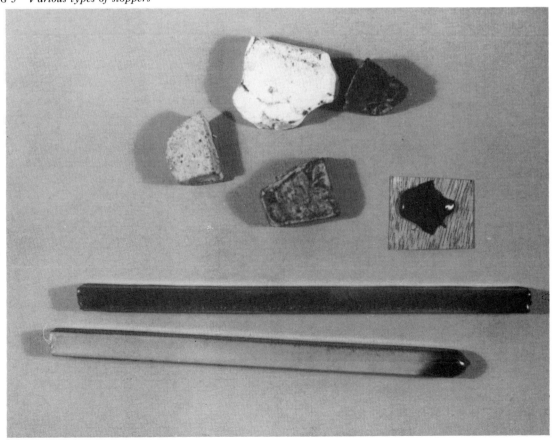

To be able to deal with all kinds of imperfections in timber and polished surfaces keep a selection of the materials mentioned previously. The following colour mixing chart may be of some help:

Revivers

Revivers are used to clean a polished surface and therefore enhance the beauty and colour of the timber. Revivers comprise a range of materials mixed in medium. Some of the materials could be

Stopping	Colour	Solvent
Shellac	Browns, Brown Umber, Vandyke Brown	Methylated spirit
Shellac	Reds, Venetian Red	Methylated spirit
Shellac	Yellows, Yellow Ochre	Methylated spirit
Shellac	White, Titanium Dioxide	Methylated spirit
Beeswax	Any coloured pigment to match the desired colour	White spirit
Cellulose jam	Pigmented cellulose lacquers	Cellulose thinners
	Clear cellulose lacquer	Cellulose thinners
Brummer paste	Manufactured coloured pigments in all shades: oak, mahogany, walnut, teak, white, black, etc	Water
Fine sawdust and glue size or PVA	Any coloured pigment	Water

Most stoppers will take some form of stain or colour. With a little skill and mixing of selected materials you can usually come up with a stopper which will be acceptable to the job in hand. Preparation of any surface is most important before any further finishing procedures are undertaken.

fine abrasives, water, paraffin, methylated spirits, linseed oil, vinegar, chalks, silicones and soft waxes. You can purchase ready made revivers, which are usually in cream form and clean much better than a wax-type liquid because wax leaves behind a deposit on the surface. Never use a wax cleaner and cream cleaner together. You will only

FIG 6   *Melting wax stopper into a bruise*

FIG 7   *Removing surplus wax stopper by sanding*

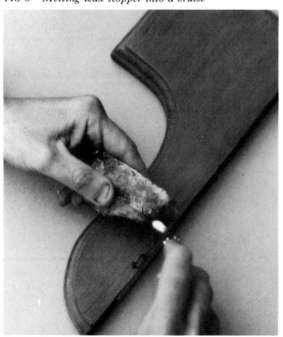

22

create a thick smudged surface. A further point to remember is that most surfaces tend to rub up and become glossy after repeated burnishing with waxes or creams. There are matt abrasives which could help in these situations, but use them with care. You can just use a damp cloth to wipe over a matt finish.

A good standard reviver used by polishers over the years is made up of equal parts of linseed oil, methylated spirits, vinegar and 14 g ($\frac{1}{2}$ oz) each of butter of antimony and camphor. Sometimes a little paraffin is also added. The reviver is shaken well and applied to the polished surface with a soft muslin cloth. Work the reviver in small circles over the polished surface and then remove the surplus reviver with a soft clean cloth or soft duster.

When using a reviver which contains silicon a silicon deposit is left on the polished surface, which becomes very difficult to remove. Constant use of these silicon revivers usually means that a polished surface may eventually need stripping completely.

Any polished surface which is resistant to heat and water could be simply revived with ordinary soap and water. The polyurethane and modified cellulose surfaces are two examples. Provided a quick reviving with a soft cream is undertaken afterwards, no problems should arise and will thus leave the polished surface clear, bright and dry.

Strippers

Most stripping solutions are produced in strong solvent form and are highly toxic. The main problem when stripping a surface coating is to determine the nature of the particular coating. Simple solvent tests can be undertaken, and the use of methylated spirits on French polish or cellulose thinners on nitrocellulose will determine the nature of the surface coating. Some surface coatings, however, are difficult to recognise by a simple solvent test. Polyurethane and polyester, for example, will not dissolve with a simple solvent because they are thermo-setting resins. These coatings require strong stripping solutions in order to soften and remove them.

One of the traditional strippers is caustic soda which being water-based tends to destroy the joints in some timber furniture, especially pine. The water dissolves the animal-based glue together with the burning action of the caustic soda. The solution tends to foam up in the joints. Repeated washing in clean water is required to wash out all the caustic soda. One point worth remembering is that the caustic soda solutions tend to darken some timbers and are not really suitable for stripping clear finishes.

The solvent and wax-type strippers are commonly used. They are usually a mixture of methylene chloride and wax and are applied liberally to the polished surface with the wax helping to contain the solvent so that it dissolves the polish.

Nowadays there are also paste strippers, some of which are very powerful and can be less messy to use than solvent-type strippers. They are simply left on the polished surface and then finally scraped or washed off. They are, however, quite expensive.

It is essential to clean all the stripping residue from the timber surface. This is best done by plenty of washing in water, methylated spirits or possibly a mild detergent. However, it is advisable in some cases to use methyl-ethyl-ketone which usually penetrates deep into open grain timbers in order to remove finally any wax residue which may have been difficult to remove with normal cleaning materials. A fine wire brush or a scrubbing brush may also be useful for cleaning.

Always take the necessary precautions of personal safety by using rubber gloves, aprons, and when stripping in internal areas use a face mask. If any stripping solution is splashed on the skin or eyes, wash off immediately with cold water. If the contamination is severe, seek medical advice. There are many proprietary strippers on the market now and it is advisable to read the instructions carefully before attempting to use them.

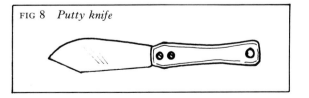

FIG 8 *Putty knife*

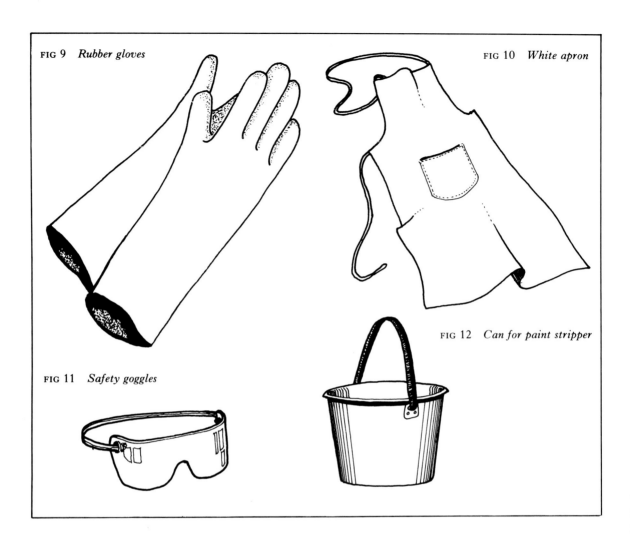

FIG 9 *Rubber gloves*

FIG 10 *White apron*

FIG 11 *Safety goggles*

FIG 12 *Can for paint stripper*

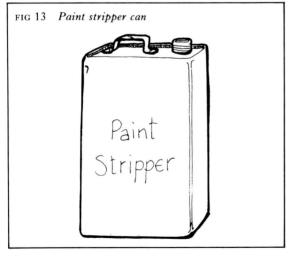

FIG 13 *Paint stripper can*

Brushes

Brushwork in woodfinishing demands a great deal of skill in the selection and use of brushes. There is a wide range of brushes on the market.

Traditionally the woodfinisher used a selection of brushes for specific purposes. The brushes have different names – colour brushes, pencil brushes, dabbers, stain brushes, stripping brushes, grass brushes, polish mops, varnish mops, wire brushes, scrubbing brushes, hog hair brushes and stipple brushes.

The composition of the brush is important: hairs can be a mixture of animal hairs, some of which are badger, bear, camel, goat, horse, pig, sable, skunk, squirrel, and also some vegetable

24

fibres, which could be bass, cane, coco and mexican fibre. Modern synthetic fibres are becoming increasingly popular, especially for decorating.

To produce a good quality brush it is desirable to use the best bristle, and for some brushes boar, hog, and pig hairs (bristles) are used. A good brush must be strong, flexible, durable and quite stable. The ends of bristles tend to split, which will make the brush soft and ideal for good, smooth clean work. There are many cheaper quality brushes on the market which are made from a mixture of inferior materials such as Mexican fibre, badger, ox hair, camel hair and grey squirrel. However, just because they are inferior to bristle bushes it does not mean that they do not produce good work. These brushes are suited for particular work, notably for applying French polishes, shellac varnishes, spirit colours, thin lacquers, lining and writing work.

It is important to use the correct brush for each particular skill. Here is a list of uses for each brush previously mentioned:

Type	Size*	Material application
Colour brushes	No 2–8	Spirit polish colours
Pencil brushes	No 1–6	Spirit polish colours
Dabbers	No 6–8	Spirit polish colours
Stain brushes	1 in–3 in	Oil stains
Stripping brushes	2 in–3 in	Water/solvent-based strippers (not caustic)
Grass brushes	2 in–3 in	Bleaching agents, oxalic and 2 pack solutions
Polish mops	No 4–16	French polishes and shellac varnishes
Varnish mops	oval shape (large size)	Oil-based varnishes (quality work)
Wire brushes	1 in–$\frac{1}{2}$ in width	Cleaning out grain when stripping or opening the grain in oak for liming
Scrubbing brushes	2 in–3 in	When stripping with caustic soda or washing off bleaching agents
Hog hair brushes	Flat liner or small round	For applying paints or dyes when cutting in or lining
Stipple brushes	Small stubby circular	For applying coloured marking dyes

*The numbers stated, for example 1–6, are an indication of the size of the brush and are normally stamped on the brush handle.

The storing and treatment of brushes

Brushes are usually neglected and ruined. They are, however, expensive and should be cared for properly. When a new brush is to be used it is advisable to work out the loose hairs on an old piece of timber. There are always a few loose hairs which require removing in a new brush but if the hairs continue to fall out after the initial working, then the brush is probably a cheap one. This type of brush should not be used on good quality work.

When storing varnish brushes it is advisable to put them in linseed oil. This will help to keep the bristles supple. Always wash out the oil before use. Brushes which are used in water soluble materials should be flushed out in clean water to remove any colouring matter. They can then be stored in a clean dry area – maybe a drawer or cupboard. Brushes which have been used in polish materials which are shellac-based can be left set in shellac polish or simply washed out in methylated spirits; keep them in shape by lying them down flat. Never leave them standing in any container. Scrubbing brushes and grass brushes should be thoroughly washed out in water, then dried out and stored dry.

A general purpose cleaner for brushes is a mixture of detergent and hydrocarbon which will release the heavy pigment particles in the brush; the brush will then require a good washing in clean water. However, some modern finishes are more difficult to remove from brushes, such as polyurethane resin. The resins set very hard and if they are not cleaned out properly they will ruin the brush. A good method of cleaning is to use xylol/alcohol cleaner mixed 50:50. A final washing in hot water should clean out the brush ready for further use.

Remember, brushes are expensive and should be cared for in such a way that any other person wishing to use them should be able to do so immediately. I have a small set of brushes which are 15 years old, well used, and are as good now as when they were first bought.

FIG 14   *Applying stripper on a polished surface*

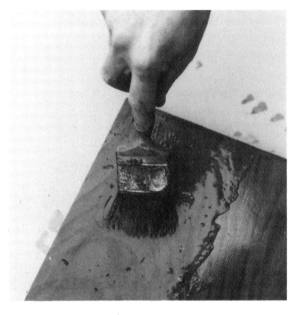

FIG 15   *Removing the softened polish with a paint scraper*

FIG 16   *Scrubbing the surface with steelwool after scraping*

FIG 17   *Neutralizing the surface with solvent after using steelwool*

FIG 18   *Paint scrapers of varying blade sizes*

FIG 19   *Brushes (from left to right): Pencil brush, B: colour brush, C: No 10 mop, D: No 12 Mop, E: stain brush*

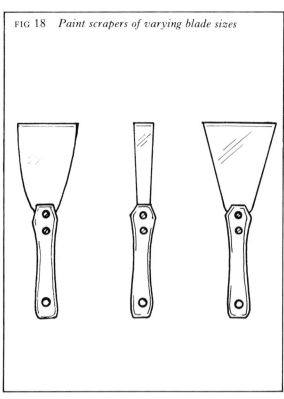

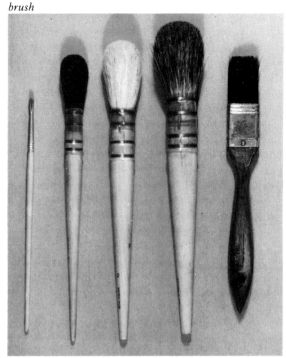

FIG 20   *Wire brush*

FIG 21   *Scrubbing brush*

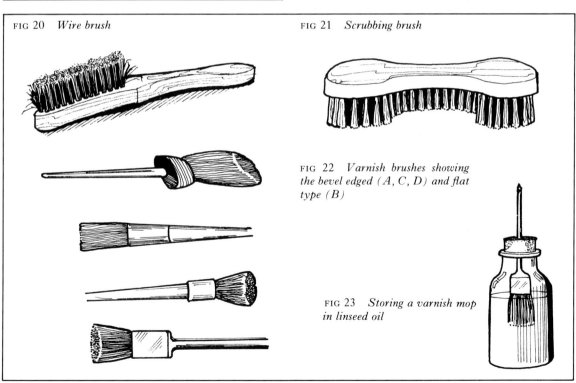

FIG 22   *Varnish brushes showing the bevel edged (A, C, D) and flat type (B)*

FIG 23   *Storing a varnish mop in linseed oil*

CHAPTER TWO

Timber preparation

●

To achieve a really good stained and polished surface on timber, it is essential to adopt a system of timber preparation. It is highly unlikely that all cabinet work made in the cabinet maker's shop is adequately prepared. There are usually a variety of marks on the timber which could be any of the following: plane marks, scratches, small dents, glue marks, open knots, shakes in the timber or veneer surfaces, unfilled panel-pin holes, or bruises. These defects must be carefully removed if they are not to be seen more clearly when stained or polished.

Scraping timber surfaces

When scraping timber surfaces use a good steel scraper. These are about 120×60 mm $(5\frac{5}{16} \times 26\frac{10}{16}$ in)and 20 swg in thickness. However, you can make your own scraper from old tenon saw blades. They can be cut and sharpened to suit your need. The long edges of the scraper are sharpened to form the cutting edge by you drawing the edge backwards and forwards along a sharpening stone to flatten and smooth the edge of the steel. When this is done you can turn over each side of the flattened edges to create a raised, sharp edge by using a scraper sharpener. Some craftsmen use a file to rough up the scraper edge before using a sharpening stone. This sharpening exercise must be practised in order to achieve a good cutting edge. The cutting edge needs to be sharp to enable a good shave of timber to be cut. When using the scraper at any angle between 45° and 70° to the wood surface, using both hands, with the thumbs facing each other at the back of the scraper. Use a steady forward movement, with even pressure, to remove a thin shaving from the timber. Always try to cut in the direction of the grain.

Normally, plane marks can be scraped out with a scraper, but further preparation is necessary to complete the removal of plane marks. This is done by a good sanding down with abrasive papers.

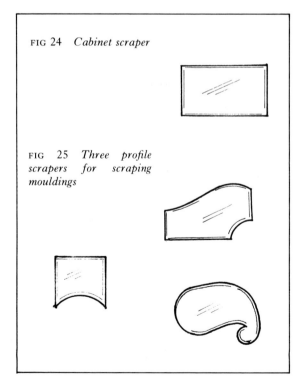

FIG 24 *Cabinet scraper*

FIG 25 *Three profile scrapers for scraping mouldings*

FIG 26   *Scraping out a scratch with a cabinet scraper*   FIG 27   *A bruise in oak timber*

Sweating out a bruise

Sweating out is a method used to remove fine and deep bruises in a timber surface. The method adopted is to swell the fibres of the timber by applying water with an old cloth over the bruised area. This operation may have to be done several times to ensure that the bruise is removed. However, to complete the job a hot iron is needed to swell the fibres of the timber more rapidly. The hot iron is placed on some brown paper which in turn is laid over the bruise. The heat from the hot iron aids the swelling of the fibres and if repeated a few times should help to remove the bruise completely.

Damping down

Although not always essential, it is advisable to damp down a timber surface which is to be stained with a water stain. If this is not done the timber fibres will be raised by the water stain, thus causing a rough surface. Any further sanding after staining would remove the surface stain, leaving a patchy surface. The damping process is also a good method to adopt for machine-made mouldings which may have vibration marks on them created by the cutters. There is no need, however, to proceed with the damping down of timbers which are to be stained with oil, spirit or mixed solvent stains.

FIG 28   *Damping the bruise with water*

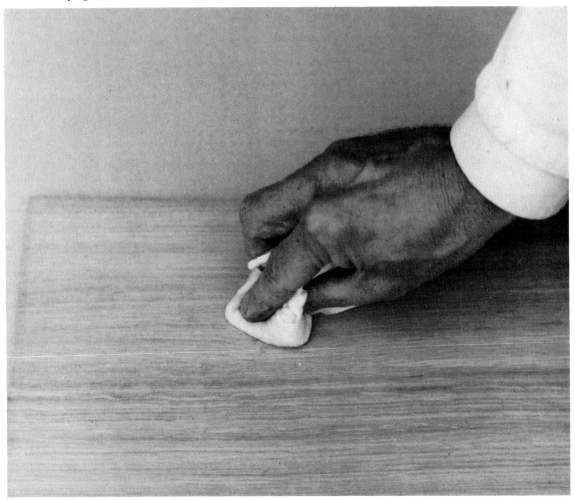

Sanding down

After the initial sweating out and damping down the timber surface must be sanded to produce a nice clean smooth surface before any staining or polishing can be undertaken. Numerous types of abrasive papers are used for this operation. Always remember to use your abrasive papers in the correct order, starting with the coarser grade then working to a finer grade for final sanding. Work with the length of the grain, doing sanding in corners of framework and mouldings in a circular motion to avoid scratches.

Finally, inspect the sanding operation by holding your work up to the light to see if there are any fine marks which still need removing. If it is carcase work, try to move the work near to a good direction of light.

Sometimes you will come across glue marks which are unsightly and require removal. This defect can be due to bad gluing with insufficient removal of surplus glue or to glue perforation which usually shows itself on glued veneers. With modern synthetic glues this can be a problem because if the glue is not removed, then no staining can take place as glues are not reversible and show themselves as unsightly marks on the timber surface.

If continuous sanding must be done use a

FIG 29 *Sweating out the bruise using a hot iron over brown paper*

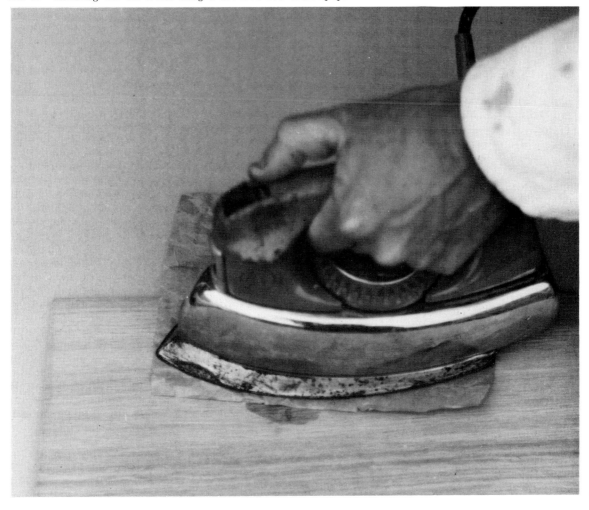

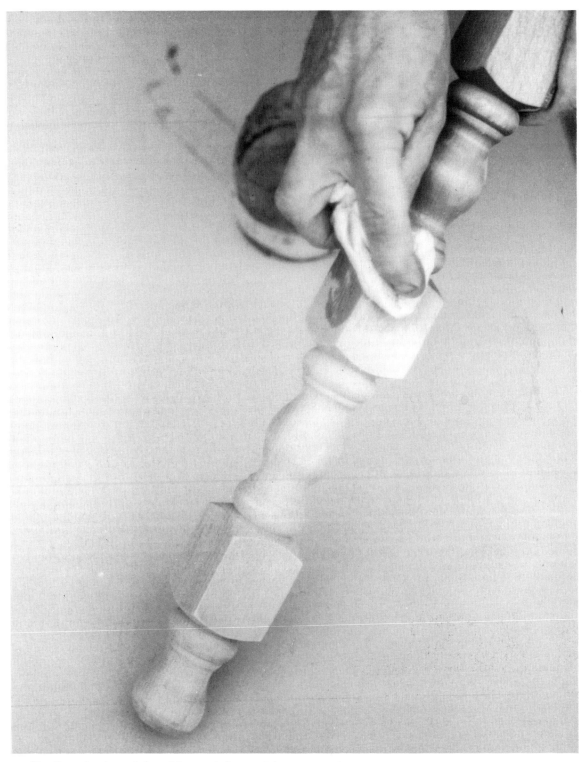

FIG 30 *Damping down timber with water before applying water stain*

32

FIG 31   *Sanding with garnet paper and a cork block*

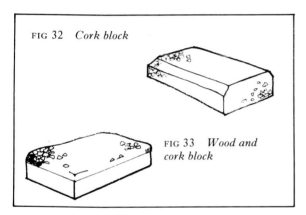

FIG 32   *Cork block*

FIG 33   *Wood and cork block*

portable sander and wear a face mask for safety purposes. Some sanding dust can be very irritating and could be a health hazard. Of course, for smaller flat surfaces a cork sanding block is all that is needed.

When choosing an abrasive paper for a particular job, it is best to check the grit size and type of paper. Traditional abrasive papers are numbered from No 0 up to No 3. These grades used to relate to the old glasspapers which have now been replaced by the much better garnet papers. Garnet papers can be graded by the numbers 7/0, 6/0, 5/0 and 4/0 and they cut much cleaner and last much longer than glasspapers. Other types of papers may also be used and one such paper is silicone carbide, which is usually described as wet or dry, simply because it can be used with water as well as in its dry state. It is not advisable to use this abrasive in its wet state on timbers. It is normally used on paintwork, on both timbers and metalwork.

One other abrasive is the lubrisil type which is designed to create lubrication whilst sanding. A fine chalk is incorporated in the face of the abrasive paper so that a smooth cut is obtained whilst the cutting action of the abrasive takes place. This abrasive is normally used on polished surfaces.

A good tip when sanding moulding work is to cut a reverse mould so that you can use this like a sanding block. Also, always store your abrasive papers in a dry, warm place and when your abrasive papers become clogged up with sanding dust, shake the dust out by tapping the paper on the edge of the workbench. Wet or dry papers can simply be washed out in clean water.

With the large variety of abrasive papers available, it is not always easy to select the correct abrasive for each job. However, by carefully considering the work in hand it is possible to choose a good selection of abrasives and finish with a satisfying well-sanded job. A well-prepared timber surface will reap benefits with further processes in finishing at a later stage.

33

CHAPTER THREE

Staining

———————•

Choosing the correct colour of stain may help you to provide a good colour effect on cheaper timbers. The stain chosen could have the effect of producing a good oak, walnut or mahogany colour, for example. Obviously it is best to study the nature of timbers in detail so that you can understand how selected timbers can react with the application of stains. Traditionally, timbers such as oak, walnut and mahogany would have been used, but because of the expense of these timbers nowadays substitute timbers are often used and are then stained to give the colour of a traditional timber. A well-stained piece of timber is attractive, and there is no reason why, if stained properly, the work should not look good. The art of staining for amateurs and in some cases tradesmen can often be poor owing to ignorance or complete disregard for essential details in basic stain application. There is nothing worse than a badly stained piece that has been polished, thus showing the uneven stain application. (NB Don't confuse staining with painting. They are entirely different concepts.)

Staining timber brings out the beauty and nature of the grain. The different densities of grains of timbers enable various shade effects and contrasts to be produced; these effects come about owing to the varying degrees of absorption of colouring agent in different parts of the grain structure. Having a good eye for colours will help you select your shade and produce a suitably pleasing effect.

Hardwoods were usually used for cabinet making, and the timbers mentioned earlier were prominent many years ago. However, owing to high timber costs we now make furniture of veneers, which are laid on chipboard and sometimes on medium density fibre board surfaces. Normally the cabinet maker will use solid timbers for the carcase construction together with other alternative timbers. If there are carvings to be produced, then use good carving timbers. These timbers must match the rest of the work and they are usually white timbers such as oak, lime, pine or also the fruitwoods. Staining carvings usually makes them look antique in colour and they are ideal for producing reproduction furniture which at the present time seems to be becoming readily acceptable.

You will find that the white timbers need to be stained to obtain the desired effect. The current trend is to stain mahogany and oak timbers with teak; pine is also popular but is coloured in a light shade. The skill of the woodfinisher and the use of stains with a range of modern dyes can produce so many different colours on selected timbers that it is difficult to imagine the results without producing colour samples first. It must be pointed out that good colour samples are a must to appreciate the use of colour stains and dyes on timber.

Timbers for staining and polishing

Hardwoods

Beech – A light coloured timber which can also be a much redder colour owing to its acidity. Use water stains on this timber to obtain a clearer and more even effect. Normally used for chairmaking.

Birch – Produced in plywood form and not suitable for most stains other than water stains. It can look very attractive if the timber is carefully selected. A very light white timber.

Boxwood – Normally pale yellow in colour. Can be used for stringing in furniture and also handles in woodworkers' tools. Usually polished in its natural colour.

Cherry – A nicely grained timber in a warm brown colour. Polishes well in its natural colour but can be stained.

Elm – The English variety is used for chair seats and frames and is now often found in furniture made from selected veneers. Light brown in col-our. Can be stained with oil stains and suitable as a substitute for oak. Tends to warp but has an attractive grain.

Ebony – A very rare timber nowadays of African origin and, although very dark brown, can have pale yellow, white and even greenish streaks. Used often as a veneer on cabinet work, for toning and sometimes jewellery boxes. Can be polished, natural or even stained black.

Harewood – A sycamore timber which is dyed by the vacuum chemical process to produce a grey colour. Can be polished in its greyish tone or tinted down a little with tinted polishes or waxes.

Iroko – Dark yellowish brown, often mistaken for teak and darkens with age. Can be used for some cabinet work but is really more frequently

FIG 34 *Examples of board materials (from top to bottom): pine faced blockboard, mahogany faced blockboard, laminboard, plywood, chipwood*

used for garden furniture and laboratory work-benches. It is very strong, and can be oiled or oil stained. Good for finishing with urethane varnishes.

Kingwood – A South American timber which is dark brown in colour with streaks of crimson red, violet and purple. A fine grained timber. Normally used as a veneer in cabinet work. Polished in it natural state.

Laburnum – A good hardwood both for turning and polishing. Can take a good oil stain. Dark brown in colour.

Mahogany – Various varieties of mahogany including African (brown in colour), Cuban, Honduras, Brazilian and Spanish which is grown in the San Domingo region. Probably one of the most popular timbers used in furniture production, it is easily stained with either water, oil or mixed solvent stains. A variety of reddish pink colours in its natural state. The timber is open grained and polishes really well with most surface coatings.

Makore – An extremely sensitive timber to light and is a figured brown colour. Takes oil stains and polishes easily.

Maple – Used to be a very popular timber for veneer work in cabinet making. A figured variety known as birdseye maple was used for decorating the old railway carriages. A pale white colour sometimes with a creamish tint and was also used for ballroom dance floors. A very hard wearing timber. Not always stained but polished natural.

Oak – Another very popular timber for furniture manufacturing both in solid and veneer form. Very strong and lightish brown in colour. Takes any stain and polishes really well with all types of surface coatings. Because of its acid content it tends to like chemical stains that are used to produce special antique colours.

Obeche – A pale yellow colour, it was used to imitate mahogany and stains quite well. Tends to bruise easily, however.

Padauk – A dark crimson coloured timber which sometimes has black and brown streaks in it. Polishes really well and is ideal for staining. Is often used for furniture and as a decorative effect in some large public buildings. Well used in America.

Purpleheart – An excellent timber for turning which has a good lustre. Polishes and stains really well. A hard purple coloured timber.

Rosewood (Rio and Bahia) – Both are grown in Brazil, but the Bahia rosewood is reputed to be the better. Dark reddish brown in colour with dark brown and black streaks, the greater colour being a purple base with a rose-like scent. Products from this timber include cabinet work, veneers and—many years ago—pianos, which were, amazingly, often polished black. A very scarce timber, expensive (£200 per cube at the time of writing) but stains and polishes really well.

Rosewood (Indian) – Much darker than the Brazilian types and used for cabinet work, it is currently exported to the United Kingdom in furniture styles of the 1930s. Usually polished in its natural colour.

Sycamore – A close textured timber which is pale whitish-yellow but tends to discolour. It has a slight ripple figure and is agreeable with some bright water stain colours. Often it is used for interior linings in some cabinet work and is then polished in its natural colour.

Sapele – Very common in the 1960s. A pale pinkish brown colour which stains well with oil stains. Well used in the furniture trades and building industry for panelled doors.

Satinwood – A golden yellow colour that is finely figured and tends to darken with age. Polishes really well in its natural colour but can be stained if so desired. Only used for the most exquisite cabinet work, panelling and specialist veneer work.

Teak (Indian, Burmese and Bangkok) – A yellow brown wood which changes colour on ageing. Having its own oil, it can simply be oiled over and needs little care. A very strong, durable timber which can be lightly stained with golden tints to enhance its beauty. Recommended surface coatings are polyurethane, oils and waxes. Now widely used in furniture manufacturing.

Tulip wood – Another Brazilian timber commonly used in traditional furniture for inlay work and some marquetry work. Polished in its natural state.

Tupelo – An American timber that tends to warp but is used for some furniture parts. A pale creamy yellow colour which discolours on exposure to light. Sometimes used instead of normal whitewoods and can be stained with water or oil stains.

Walnut – A commonly grown timber in Europe that is greyish brown in colour. Has a really good figure and is excellent for oil staining. Good for cabinet work, pianos and some carving. Very difficult to work, needs skill. Polishes to a high lustre and looks brilliant in a high gloss finish.

Walnut (black) – Grown in North America and is more straight grained and durable. Much darker in colour than European walnut and looks well polished dark or stained dark. Likes oil stains. There are also African and Australian walnuts but these are not generally classed as walnuts in the true sense. Italian walnut is very highly figured and was used in the 1930s for quarter veneer work on much English cabinet work and was stained and polished to a warm brown colour.

Yew – This timber is normally a rich amber and derives from Europe and India. It can sometimes be reddish brown and is often well figured. A close grained hard wood, its main use is for veneers and decorative work, furniture and chair frames.

Zebra wood – A very hard Indian timber with a reddish brown colour, having dark red or brown streaks. Sometimes used for making handles for tools and some decorative work.

Softwoods

Canarywood (whitewood) – Yellow in colour, this wood sometimes has dark marks in it. It changes colour in light and was often used in the early 1920s for cheap furniture. Polishes and stains quite well.

Cedar – Cedar is an outdoor timber that has a reddish brown colour with a scented smell. Its different varieties include West Indian, Himalayan, Atlantic and Cedar of Lebanon and it is usually used for fine cabinet work, furniture and some carvings.

Pine – Many varieties of this timber are widely used including baltic, scots pine, yellow pine, pitch pine and parana pine. The colours vary from white through yellow to pale pink and it is usually used for construction purposes in carpentry and joinery. The wood is often polished in its natural colour or stained.

Douglas fir – A nicely grained timber which is strong and resinous. It is good for staining to look aged in kitchens, cafes and restaurants.

Chestnut – A European timber sometimes known as sweet chestnut. A light brown colour and easy to work, used for panelling and complementing oak. It can also be stained to resemble oak colours.

Poplar – Ideal for turning and making plywood, this is quite a soft and reddish brown wood. It is not often used in furniture production.

Lime – A good timber for carving, pale yellow in colour. It is used for piano keyboards, and polishes and stains well.

Satin walnut – A cheap timber from North America, it is a pale reddish colour, close grained and quite smooth. It does however, tend to twist and warp and was used extensively on cheap furniture.

The timbers referred to above are just a number available to the woodfinisher, and the list is not comprehensive. Many of the timbers mentioned can be polished in their natural state and need no staining. However, it must be emphasized that some timbers are much more attractive if stain is applied; the processes undertaken for the actual staining of timbers can now be dealt with in great detail.

Why stain timber?

Most timbers have their own natural grain beauty and can be polished without any staining at all. However, some form of colouring agent is normally used to enhance the grain. By applying this colouring agent the nature of the timber changes and the grain effect is more pronounced, becoming darker, warmer or sometimes colder. The stain applied colours the softer parts of the timber and therefore strikes fairly deeply into the wood. Different colour tones are produced and these tones tend to enhance the natural grain.

Types of stains

Water stains

These stains are produced in a whole range of colours, but probably the most popular colours are walnut and mahogany. These two colours were used extensively for staining beech chair-frames and produce an even colour. The colouring agent is either vegetable or mineral and is soluble in water. The application of water stains will lift the grain so damp down the timber with water before applying any water stain. When the timber is dry, lightly sand down before applying the stain. There should be no further raising of the grain. If applying water stains on top of each other, allow the first coat to dry properly before applying the second coat. If you wish to dry the stain quickly use a warm radiator for speeding the drying process.

Water stains tend to be cheap, come in many colours but lack penetration. They do, however, produce even colours. There are now what are called water-pigmented stains, which are stains with heavy colouring agents composed of micro-fine pigments. These pigments tend to produce a more opaque colour to the wood and therefore have less clarity. Do not, however, use water stains on oily timbers such as teak. Oily timbers tend to produce a patchy colour effect when stained with water.

A further water staining treatment is known as size staining or water coating. This method is used on cheap timbers and incorporates the use of colours ground in water, such as ochres, umbers and chromes. This type of stain, however, produces a blinding out effect on the timber – that is, the grain is obliterated. This stain is ideal for backs of cabinets, especially those made of ply-wood and cheap grade timbers.

Timbers ideal for water staining – are: walnut, beech, lime, sycamore, mahogany birch, poplar, ash, whitewood, elm, pine, and alder.

Spirit stains

These stains are one of the traditional stains used for tinting mahoganies but are very difficult to use owing to their quick drying nature on large surfaces. The main use of spirit dyes nowadays is for tinting sealers and other stains. Spirit stains are usually aniline dyes dissolved in methylated spirit. The colours can be derived from aniline powders, dyestuffs, vegetable products and metallic salts. Many colours are produced including red, green, blue, black, mauve, pink and yellow.

Timbers ideal for spirit staining – are: Mahogany, African walnut, whitewood, rosewood, satin walnut, and obeche.

Oil stains

Probably the most widely used stains in the wood-finishing trade owing to the ease with which they can be applied. The colouring matter usually derives from coal tar and bitumen products which can include tinting by adding other oil soluble dyes. Oil stains are used extensively on hardwoods, and, because they tend to be slow drying, it is best to allow them an adequate length of drying time before any further process takes place. The minimum length of drying time should be one hour, preferably two.

The solvents for these stains are naphtha and other petroleum products and can be thinned down with white spirit. With the use of more finely dispersed pigments we now have a much better light fastness in colour but with less clarity. Oil stains penetrate the fibres of wood very well and produce very rich colours, especially in brown shades on oak timbers. A variety of oil stain colours are produced, the standard colours being black, mahogany, walnut, oak and red.

Timbers ideal for oil staining – are: oak, elm, afrormosia, walnut, ash, African walnut, mahogany, rosewood, sapele, iroko, merranti and utile.

Mixed solvent stains

These are fast drying and often known as NGR stains (non-grain-raising). They are formulated on the light fast soluble dyestuffs with added alcohol and naphtha. One fault with these stains is that they sometimes lift or bleed into the polish. However, owing to the fast drying properties it means that there is no drying time and consequently you may proceed to seal the stain almost immediately.

Non-grain-raising stains (NGR)

True NGR stains are a water soluble acid dye

stain with a glycol ether solvent to promote fast drying. They have good penetration, are light fast and do not raise the grain. However, they are expensive and tend to form patches of colour in certain areas of the timber that can be unsightly. When sealing on NGR stains, take extra care because of the bleeding effect of the dyes in these stains. Considerable skill is required to obtain a clear, even colour. The best way to apply these stains is to use the spray method, but a rag or swab can be used with care.

Timbers ideal for mixed solvent and non-grain-raising stains – are: teak, sapele, agba, iroko, utile, afrormosia and merranti.

Chemical stains

These stains are dissolved in water, which makes them cheap, but the disadvantage is that the grain of the timber is raised. They have shallow, even penetration that gives good, even colour. The problem of selected chemical stains is that they react with the tannic acid in the timber and produce garish colours if used too strong. Some of these stains are caustic soda, bichromate of potash, American potash (potassium hydroxide) and ammonia. One other chemical that may be used is iron sulphate. This produces a very dark grey colour on acidic timbers. If no tannic acid is present in the wood, then you can apply a tannin solution before staining with a chemical.

When using chemical stains you must be very careful as the results are quite variable depending on the timber. The woodfinisher may need to make certain adjustments, and it is always best to stain some test pieces first.

The main reason for using chemical stains is to obtain special colours on choice work, such as oak panelling, church furniture and for restoring antique furniture. Probably the most commonly used timber for chemical staining is oak because of its tannic acid content. Usually a caustic soda stain is used to obtain rich brown colours. On mahogany, we use bichromate of potash, which is then sometimes oiled down to produce an old sheraton colour. This, of course, is ideal for reproduction work. Other materials that may also be used for staining are copper sulphate, slaked lime, carbonate of potash and permanganate of potash.

Whenever you decide to use chemical stains, try to choose the stain carefully; mix the stain making it fairly weak to medium in strength, and always use a test piece before proceeding with the actual work. If these stains are chosen with care and applied correctly they will produce some really brilliant, lasting colours and enhance the beauty of the grain, especially on good figured English oak and the traditional mahoganies.

Timbers ideal for chemical stains – are: English oak, Honduras mahogany, European oak, Cuban mahogany, American oak, Brazilian mahogany, English walnut and pine.

Applying stains

There are various methods of applying stains. They may be applied by brush rag, sprayed or dipped. To obtain good results when staining decide on some form of system. For someone who

FIG 35   *Applying stain working with the grain*

is fairly new to staining, it would be better to use the slower drying stains such as the oil stains. The objective in staining is to obtain a perfectly even colour without any patchy areas showing. When you are more experienced then the faster drying solvent can be used, such as the mixed solvent type.

When applying stain, always work with the grain and attempt to stain straight through your work, from left to right, keeping the edges of each application wet if possible. Try to work fairly quickly so that your stain does not dry, otherwise you may have a patchy effect. If you are working with panelled work or mouldings, try to work from the corner of the panel or moulding and wipe off the excess stain as quickly as possible so as to keep an even colour.

If you are applying stain by hand, a useful material to use is muslin. Muslin holds the stain quite stable and helps you apply an even colour. Brushes tend to release the stain too quickly, and sometimes it is difficult to control the flow of stain if you are unused to brush application. In addition, always remove the surplus stain by rubbing it off with an old rag. This will help the stain to dry out more quickly and also provide an even colour.

Normally stains are only applied by spraying if there are a number of jobs to be stained, especially chairframes. An oil stain or mixed solvent stain could be used with one person applying the stain and another wiping off the excess. If the dipping

FIG 36 *Wiping off surplus stain with the grain*

FIG 37 *Fixing the stain with a fad of polish*

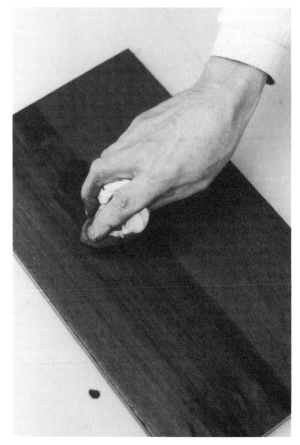

technique is used it is usually for staining small objects, such as clock cases, toys, jewellery boxes and chair legs (unfitted).

When you have completed your staining operation some areas of work may be different colours. Do not worry too much about this because you can re-stain the lighter areas. If the second stain application is still not giving you a satisfactory colour, then a later colouring operation will be required. This colouring operation will be dealt with in the book.

Finally, if the stain applied is too dark you may wash it out with a solvent. The solvent chosen will depend on the type of stain applied, so you may use water, turpentine substitute, methylated spirits or cleaning fluid if mixed solvent stains have been applied. Always allow the timber to dry before re-staining.

CHAPTER FOUR

Woodfillers

———●———

Often referred to as 'grain fillers', these are normally used under clear finishes for filling pores of the grain so that any surface coating applied will hold up on the filled surface and not sink into the wood. They help to prevent absorption of any surface coating. Woodfillers are produced in most colours, including walnut, oak, mahogany and transparent colours. Woodfillers also colour the wood, save lacquer and polish, and provide a nice clean surface for further finishing.

A woodfiller comprises mainly a filling powder, an extender, a binding agent, a colour and a solvent or some kind of medium. The most important part is the filling powder, which must be hard and have a good fine particle size. Also the filling powder must not absorb too much oil and it should not have any adverse effect on any subsequent coats of polish to the substrate.

An extender normally modifies the grain filler and makes the product cheaper. One such extender is China clay; other extenders include chalks and sometimes asbestine. These materials can help the filler to move more easily and can be wiped more easily; they also make the surface smoother, facilitating application and removal. Pigments colour the filler but sometimes a bitumen material may be used or even a tinting dye. Too much pigment, however, causes cloudy obliteration problems that will give less clarity to the wood. The use of dyes is essential for the tinting to produce a warmer or colder colour. The binding agent determines the type of filler, whether it is oil-bound, resin-bound or a catalyst-type filler.

Probably the most popular filler is the patent filler known as oil-bound. The filler usually contains either alkyd varnish, copal varnish, gold size or linseed oil in the filler formulation. These fillers are slow drying and should be allowed to dry for a minimum of four hours or longer. Obviously the drying of oil-bound fillers causes a problem in the finishing shop. In my experience, we always applied the filler in the afternoon so that there was adequate overnight drying and the work was ready for sealing the next morning. Nowadays synthetic resins are used that eliminate the slow-drying oils, thus allowing the fillers to dry much faster. These fillers are classed as resin-bound fillers but are much more difficult to apply.

Resin-bound fillers were designed to be used under catalyst-type lacquers, giving a much harder base to work on. Such finishers as polyurethane and polyester were used on resin-bound fillers. However, owing to the short pot life it became difficult to apply. We used to use two people, one to apply the filler and one to remove the surplus, and this was usually successful. However, these fillers are very stable and fill the grain adequately; they also give good stability and good adhesion to the wood surface and any further coats of lacquer.

Solvents are used simply to carry the solids and traditionally we used turpentine or white spirit. The resin-bound fillers use xylol or naphthalene.

Certain other fillers are worth a mention and these are the traditional fillers which were used well before the more modern types used today.

Traditional woodfillers

Plaster of Paris
A good filler, very old and quite stable. When applying it prepare the plaster and water beforehand. Dip your rag into the water, then the plaster, apply to the wood surface rubbing well into the grain in a circular motion, and then quickly remove the surplus with a clean rag, taking care not to remove any plaster from the grain. Allow to dry for as long as possible, at least an hour, then paper off the surplus. After papering, apply a thin coating of linseed oil to remove the whiteness or alternatively use a pigment colour that will cancel out the whiteness. This type of filler was commonly used in Victorian times on chairs, which probably produced a yellowish white effect as the grain showed through the polish. It is advisable to use this type of filler only under French polish and not under any modern surface coatings.

Limed oak filler
A very popular filler during the 1930s on oak furniture. It shows itself by a white deposit in the grain. Usually the timber would have been selected for its good figure. The filler consisted of the base formulation but with added titanium oxide white to make the filler more pronounced. This filler was rubbed into the grain and cleaned off. A substitute white used was flake white.

Decorative coloured filler
By using a standard transparent filler you can use dry pigments to provide a bright coloured filler. By adding green, blue, yellow or any other colour you can obtain a decorative coloured grain effect in open grain timbers such as oak, ash, elm or teak. The normal procedure is to seal the wood with white polish, allow to dry, lightly paper down, then apply the filler and remove the surplus, wiping across the grain. You may apply stain if you desire a darker background colour but this would be done before any sealing.

Polish fillers
Before modern fillers became popular, the woodfinisher would simply use polish as a filler. If the work had been stained a thin sealing coat would have been applied with rubber, allowed to dry, then lightly papered down. Apply a good coat of heavy bodied polish with a polishing mop and allow to dry thoroughly. Paper down again to provide a smooth surface, dust off and apply several rubbers of thinned polish to work out a flat polished surface and simultaneously force the polish into the pores of the wood surface. Allow this polish to harden off for about three or four hours and then repeat the process again. You can get a good flat surface by using a little pumice powder inside your rubber in order to flatten the polished surface. Care must be taken not to apply too much pumice inside the rubber.

Homemade woodfillers
If you want to make your own fillers it is better to use a basic transparent filler and the particular pigment colour you desire. Below are some examples of basic coloured woodfillers for selected timbers.

Traditional woodfiller application
Before modern woodfillers were used woodfinishers relied on local materials to fill in the

Wood	Type of filler and pigment
Ash	Transparent oil-bound filler; add yellow ochre or brown umber for oak colours
Elm	Transparent oil-bound filler; add brown umber, vandyke brown, yellow ochre or a little orange chrome with a brown depending on warmth of colour required
Mahogany	Transparent oil-bound filler; with vandyke brown, brown umber and a little red oil stain
Oak	Transparent oil-bound filler; with brown umber, yellow ochre or gas black for antique oak, jacobean or tudor oak
Walnut	Transparent oil-bound filler; add turkey umber, brown umber or a mixture of orange chrome, vandyke brown and yellow ochre for a warm walnut
Rosewood	Transparent oil-bound filler; add rose pink with brown umber

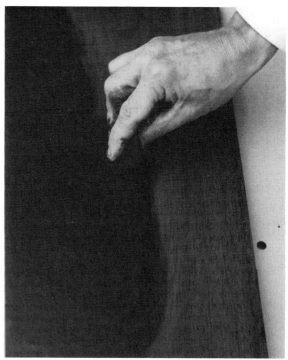

FIG 38   *Mixing woodfiller before application*
FIG 39   *Applying woodfiller in a circular motion*
FIG 40   *Removing the surplus woodfiller rubbing across the grain*

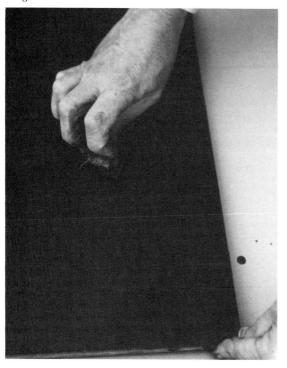

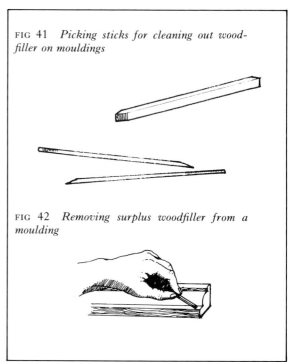

FIG 41   *Picking sticks for cleaning out woodfiller on mouldings*

FIG 42   *Removing surplus woodfiller from a moulding*

grain pores. These materials consisted of pumice powder, ground glass, ground brick dust and pigments such as umbers, ochres, to provide colour. These materials would be ground in oils and rubbed into the pores of the wood. Whilst filling the grain, these materials would also have the effect of smoothing down the wood surface because of their abrasive nature. As we now use more modern and quicker drying materials in the manufacture of woodfillers we have to adopt a good method of application.

Woodfillers should be applied with an old rag in a circular motion across the grain. The surplus filler should then be wiped off with old hessian or canvas. Always wipe off the surplus filler across the grain of the wood, using fairly heavy pressure. Finally, using an old rag clean off again, rubbing hard, and you should have a good clean filled surface. Points to remember are apply fillers only on small areas at a time, about 300 mm^2 (12 sq in) and remove the surplus filler before proceeding to the next area. Even though woodfillers are oil-based they do dry fairly quickly, especially in warm conditions. Only apply sufficient woodfiller to enable the grain to be filled. Remember, the more filler you apply, the more you need to remove – try to apply just enough. After the surplus removal you should try to allow the filler to dry out as long as possible so that you can obtain the best results. If you can allow the filler to dry overnight, then do so.

Finally, it must be emphasized that only open grain timbers are normally filled, and if any colouring of close grain timbers is required it is usually done by applying stains. A final point is that woodfillers can be applied directly over stains.

CHAPTER FIVE

French polishing

●

Since early Victorian times most of the furniture produced in this country was French polished, and thus there is a great deal of furniture available which now requires refinishing or partially restoring. During the Victorian era the trade of French polishing was at its height and therefore there were many skilled French polishers available to polish all types of furniture. In this chapter I shall attempt to provide the reader with the necessary information required to overcome the problems of French polishing a range of furniture items.

The term French polish is a comprehensive one and there are a number of different types of polishes manufactured by the suppliers, each with their own trade names. The most commonly known names are: French polish, button polish, garnet polish, white polish and transparent polish and they are each slightly different.

French polish

This is a basic polish which contains methylated spirit and shellac. The amount of shellac could vary from 1–3 kg (2–6 lb) 5 litres (7½ pt) and is referred to as the 'cut' – thus a 'two pound cut'. The colour of the polish will depend on the type of shellac used but in this case it is usually a mid-brown colour. Nowadays one of the most popular solvents used to make French polish is ethyl alcohol. Other materials may also be added to provide special properties. For example, gum benzoin to give good brilliance or damar resin to provide heat resistance, and coloured spirit soluble dyes to produce black or red polishes. If a basic polish sealer is required then French chalk or stearates may be added to promote sanding properties.

French polish can be used under most surface coatings providing the polish is allowed to dry sufficiently. It is ideal to use French polish to act as a buffer coat between dyes which might bleed under later coats of lacquer if finally applying a modern finish. The surface produced by French polishing is vulnerable, thermoplastic and reversible so it can be quite easily attacked by heat, moisture and spirit. However, if the work is adequately polished it produces a very pleasing appearance which will enhance the beauty of the grain.

Button polish

A much brighter colour than the traditional French polish, less cloudy and not quite as waxy. It is made by crushing button shellac, which is diluted in methylated spirit. It has a bright warm brown colour ideal for polishing mid-brown shades on oak, walnut and mahogany. This polish can be used for other timbers also.

Garnet polish

Made from garnet lac. A true dark polish with a golden tint ideal for dark walnuts and dark oaks needing a special tinting colour. It needs a certain amount of skill to avoid patchy polishing. Must be applied evenly.

White polish

Normally used for very light timbers such as ash, sycamore, lime and light oak (natural). Produced by dissolving bleached or white lac in methylated spirits. Because of the bleaching agents used in the bleached white polish, this type of polish tends to be somewhat soft when dried out completely and therefore is quite vulnerable to normal domestic use.

Transparent polish

Pale shellacs are used to produce this grade of polish and it is normally used for final polishing to give a good brilliant finish. This polish can also be used instead of white polish, if this is not available, but will produce a very pale tinted yellow effect on light timbers similar to those mentioned in white polish.

In conclusion it must be mentioned that if coloured polishes are required other than those mentioned above, spirit soluble dyes can be used to produce tinted polishes. These polishes should be well strained for clarity. If solid colours are required then the pigments, which must also be strained, can be added to the polish. The pigments will provide an obliterating coloured polish which would be ideal for covering unwanted colours in timbers and also for giving a base colour for graining or marbling.

The polishing shop

To produce good quality work you must have a good workshop which is light, clean and dust free. The working area should always be kept as clean as possible, and the temperature should never fall below 60°F. The temperature is particularly important because any fluctuations make the polish viscous and difficult to apply.

You will require a small workbench, trestles of different sizes and a full polishing kit. Dust sheets, again of different sizes, will also be required for protecting finished items. You will also need a good selection of $\frac{1}{2}$ l ($\frac{3}{4}$ pt) and 5 l ($7\frac{1}{2}$ pt) containers to store various materials and air-tight canisters for polishing rubbers and dry pigment powders.

You will require a varied selection of rags.

These will consist of synthetic materials, old cotton sheets, old woollen blankets and polycotton shirting material. A good storage of old canvas, sacking or hessian will also come in handy for the use of woodfillers. Remember a good selection of brushes, which will include mops, pencil brushes, flat brushes, old brushes for stripping and paint kettles for the stripping solution.

Always store any abrasive materials in a dry cupboard. This also applies to any powdered materials such as dry pigments, aniline powders, pumice powder and extenders. All materials in containers should be clearly labelled. Throw out all old rags and waste materials as soon as possible after use.

The amount of material required in the workshop will depend on the size of the workshop and the amount of work produced. It is always ideal to attempt to provide plenty of space for working so that you can easily get around your work. If you can organize your workshop efficiently then this usually produces good clean work.

The polishing rubber

Now we come to the most important tool in the French polisher's kit – the polishing rubber. I have found that nearly everyone who attempts to make a polishing rubber has great difficulty doing so and controlling the rubber whilst in use. With this simple tool most of the polisher's work is produced so it is essential that the operator controls and really masters the skills of both making and using the polishing rubber. It must be emphasized that the folding of the rubber and the correct shape of the face of the rubber are part of the polisher's craft, and the failure of beginners and amateurs is usually due to the incorrect use of the rubber, which is also badly made up. So it is essential to master the craft of making a polishing rubber and the art of using it in all types of situations which you are likely to encounter.

Because you will be working on a complete range of work you will require different sizes of polishing rubbers. These can be kept in an air-tight container. Always try to keep a selection of polishing rubbers for each different coloured polish, such as garnet, button or white. When using a

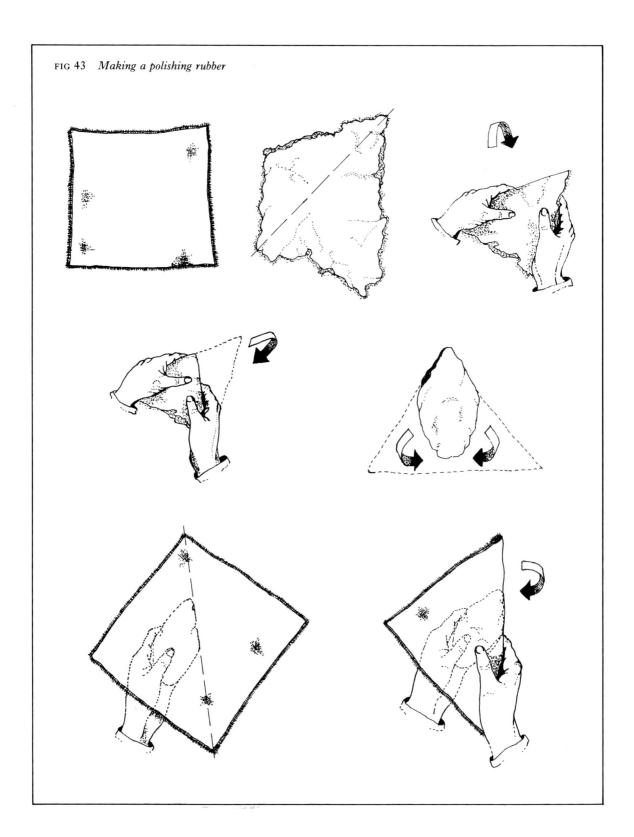

FIG 43   *Making a polishing rubber*

rubber the size of it will depend on the particular work to be undertaken – larger, for work which has a greater expanse of surface; and the smaller, for mouldings, tapered work, fretwork and wood turnings.

Making a polishing rubber

The rubber consists of two parts – the cover and the wad or fad; the former, which is made of good quality white linen or cotton fabric, covers the fad, which is made of bleached cotton wadding.

The fad holds the polish by absorption and in turn supplies the cover with polish; the cover will then distribute the polish over the surface.

The method of making up the polishing rubber is as follows.

1 Take a piece of good quality white linen or cotton fabric about 175 mm (7 in) by 125 mm (5 in).

2 Take a piece of bleached cotton wadding, the same size as the linen or cotton fabric, and fold in half. Fold in half again holding the point of the

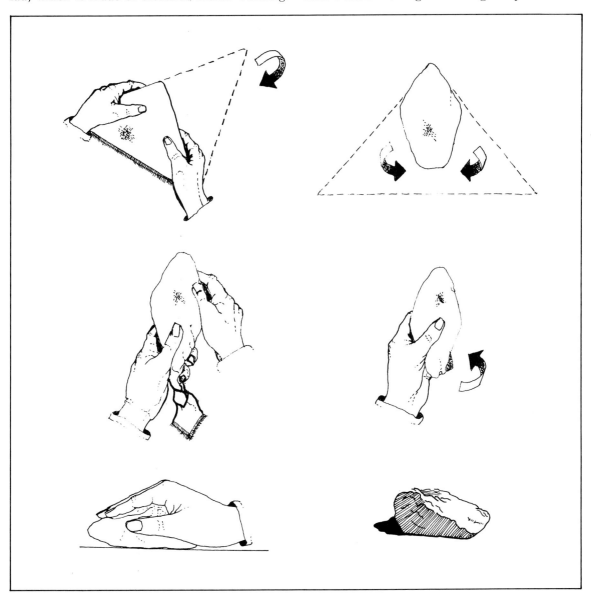

second fold with finger and thumb.

3 Fold the three remaining corners underneath to form a pear shape. This will give you the flat face of the fad.

4 Now take up your white linen or cotton fabric and holding your fad face up, place the white linen or cotton fabric over the face of the fad.

5 Hold the point of the rubber and linen together and fold under the linen on both sides.

6 Take up the loose linen and twist it round at the back of the rubber finally folding it underneath the main body of the fad. The rubber is now complete and ready for use.

Holding the rubber

1 When holding the rubber, place the forefinger on the point of the rubber on the back with the remaining three fingers at the right side (if you are right-handed).

2 It is important to hold the rubber correctly so that you can control the movement.

If you study the pictures in figure 31 carefully you will be able to construct the rubber to its correct shape and with practice making a polishing rubber will become quite easy. In no circumstances must you allow the rubber to fall out of shape. If this happens, re-make the rubber immediately—otherwise your polished work may suffer. A well-shaped rubber is absolutely essential at all times if you are to produce good quality work. Always try to keep the face of the rubber flat and free from any dirt, dust, bits of cotton or wadding. The face of the rubber delivers the polish to your work, therefore careful attention to this face is important. You may find that a hole appears in the cover of your rubber because of constant friction. All you need to do is to take off the cover and re-position the cover over the pad.

Charging the rubber with polish

Most polishers will tell you never to dip your rubber into polish. The polish is stored in small-necked bottles similar to old wine bottles or old medicine bottles with a cork inserted which has been split down the side with a vee groove. This groove allows the polish to flow from the bottle onto the pad of the rubber. To charge the rubber, take off the cover and pour a little polish on the pad from the bottle. If you are a purist you should always adopt this procedure when charging the rubber, although it is not absolutely essential. The cover will be moistened all over by exerting a little pressure to the face of the rubber by pressing with the thumb.

The amount of polish applied to the rubber should be just sufficient to make the rubber fairly wet, but not so wet that the rubber is heavy with oozing polish. If this happens, squeeze out the excess polish back into the bottle. When you have finally finished using your rubber, put it away in an airtight container. Never leave rubbers on workbenches or they will become hard, possibly dirty and useless. Your rubber is your craft tool – always look after it.

Using the rubber

Now we come to the skilled part of French polishing – applying the polish to the work. Most people have great difficulty in applying polish with a rubber and some will never master the art through being unable to control the rubber during the process. However, most people who take up polishing usually master the skills required.

With practice you will be able to produce some pleasing work; no other finish looks better than one well French polished. You must remember to practise on small work first before attempting large scale work. Don't be afraid; failure is off-putting but remember practice makes perfect so keep going and with just a little patience you will succeed. But try not to rush your work. If you study the pattern of polishing in figure 45 you will not go wrong, but remember to keep your rubber fairly moist, not too wet.

Pattern of polishing

The pattern of polishing is designed for the skilled polisher to apply the polish in a sequence so that he can obtain the best possible flat surface on his work. By careful use of the sequence the polisher will distribute the polish evenly over the work surface area and at the same time force the polish into the pores of the wood, thus filling up those pores; in the final finish the wood should have a beautifully glass-like appearance.

The method of polishing

After you have charged your rubber with polish

FIG 44   *Charging a polish rubber – follow A to C*

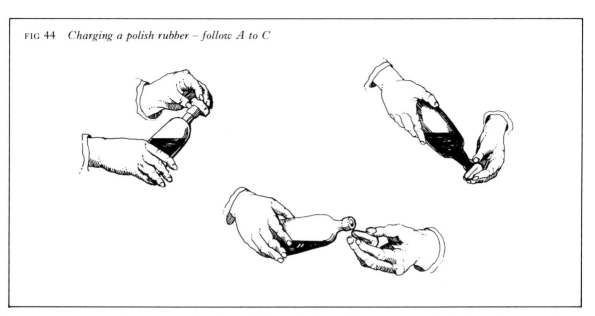

FIG 45   *The polishing sequence – follow the sequence from A to F*

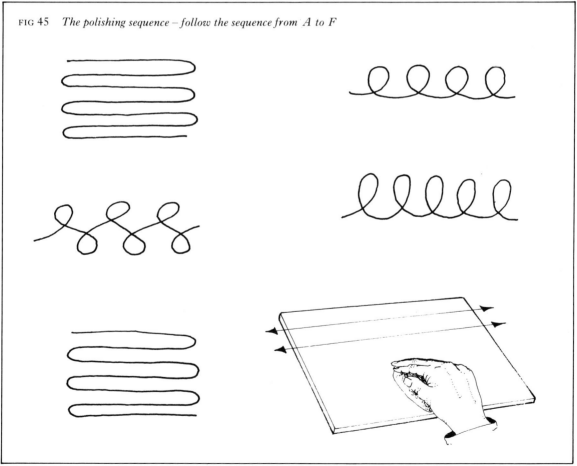

you are now ready for polishing. Firstly, apply the polish with your rubber, working from left to right with the grain of the wood using even pressure. This method seals the wood with an even coat. You can repeat this method three or four times to get a nice dull shine.

After allowing two or three minutes for the polish to dry you can now proceed to the next step. This second method is designed to fill the pores of the wood with polish. Working in circles from left to right, carefully work over the surface area of your work keeping the rubber moving; use even pressure continuously. After covering the work area two or three times, change to the third method which is to use a figure of eight pattern, again working left to right; and finally change again to an oval pattern, again working over the surface completely.

You will find this pattern of operations will obviously have to be repeated many times to enable a highly polished surface to be achieved. This is where you need the patience mentioned earlier. The work cannot be rushed because you are working with a wet material which dries slowly so you must take every care. With constant practice of polish application you will come to know how much polish you require in your rubber and the amount of pressure you need to exert to keep the polished surface flat on application.

When you are satisfied that you have obtained a good flat, highly polished surface you can finish off the work by repeating the first method of application, working your rubber from left to right.

Bodying in process

Now we have completed the basic fundamentals of polish application by rubber let us look at the main 'bodying in' process in greater detail. Normally at this stage you may have stained the timber or even filled in the grain with a woodfiller. If so the bodying in process should be a great deal easier, owing to the fact that you have a base to polish on. When bodying in you apply liberal amounts of polish to build up a fairly thick film and at the same time keep the surface as flat as possible.

The bodying in process is sometimes also known as 'bodying up'. The difference between the two is simply that bodying in is the first body of polish applied, allowed to dry for some considerable time, and then the bodying up process continues to put the final film of polish on the work. Bodying simply means that you are applying polish in film thickness over a period of time; this period will depend on how skilled you become in mastering the use of the polisher's rubber with the various polishes and the type of wood. For a complete full gloss finish the work may take hours. There is no particular set standard of finish the polisher works to. Normally a good flat surface is all that is required and it will depend on the cost of the work as to the time which may be allowed to complete a particular job.

Basically there are two finishes which the polisher uses. The 'stiffing up' process which can be used on most open grain timbers such as oak, elm or ash and the final finish which is known as open grain, semi-bodied up or partially bodied. The second process is the 'full finish', 'spirited out' or the 'acid finish', known as the 'vitriol finish' in the piano woodfinishing industry many years ago.

With the stiffing up process a thick film of polish is not required so the work is finished much more quickly and cleanly. This process is often used on a complete range of open grain timbers used in furniture, shopfittings, building fixtures and church furniture. When bodying in, however, you may come across some problems when applying your polish. If you apply too much polish with a wet rubber too quickly your work will become very wet and sticky and could be ruined.

Other problems can, occur: if you apply too much linseed oil for lubrication your work could also be too greasy and your rubber will not 'bite' on the surface. If you work with a dry rubber and insufficient polish your work will become 'ribbed' with lines along the path of your rubber. This problem happens because there is an imbalance of polish and oil, caused by the work surface being too dry; if the surface area of the film is very soft it moves around and therefore becomes uneven.

Many other faults also occur, one of which is an

uneven surface due to the incorrect distribution of polish. Polish can be distributed from the rubber causing 'whips' on the surface area shown in the form of fine lines in circular or semi-circular lines from your rubber. Try to ensure that your rubber is correctly charged with polish and never work in circular or figure of eight patterns with a very wet rubber.

During the bodying in process you must control your rubber completely at all times – this is vital. When applying the polish always supply light, even pressure with a newly charged rubber, working steadily, and increase the pressure of the rubber as the polish in the rubber decreases. If you work out most of the polish from your rubber before re-charging you should have a good hard flat surface; aim for this complete flatness at all times.

When you are satisfied that the surface is well bodied in and flat, then it is advisable to leave the work for some time to harden off. This will allow the solids to settle with solvent evaporation taking place, providing you with a good foundation for further bodying up. Always make sure your work is bright and clean, free from oil and dust before leaving to harden off.

Bodying up
The second process, that of bodying up, is used to determine what way your work will be finished. Remove any contamination from the work surface by using a dry clean rag; if any imperfections are found to be in the surface it may be necessary to lightly paper down with a fine flour paper or lubrisil paper to remove the contaminant. This light papering down is sometimes known as 'denibbing'; this removes light specks of dust or grit which may have settled and dried in the surface whilst bodying in. Another method of abrading the surface is to use a felt pad with a lubricating oil and fine pumice powder. If this method is adopted then you must clean the surface area well to remove any oily pumice after abrading. Use a clean rag.

If the final finish is going to be 'stiffed up' then you will require a good, well-shaped rubber charged with polish, which will then be lightly applied to the work surface, working from left to

right a few times. Now you begin bodying up. Apply a little linseed oil and, working in a circular motion, start to polish over the work area, again working from left to right, eventually covering the complete work area. Depending on the size of your work you may use larger sweeps of the rubber, if so desired, and at the same time light pressure.

You should charge the rubber quite frequently whilst bodying up but at the same time monitor the amount of polish you use. Remember, never use a rubber which is too wet. Control the pressure of the rubber very carefully as the work surface will be quite soft at this stage and any mistake now could prove fatal.

When you are satisfied that your work is fairly flat and sufficient polish has been applied then you may proceed to stiff up your work. Take up your rubber and working with light pressure from left to right work carefully, overlapping each stroke of the rubber until the whole surface has been covered. Make sure that each stroke comes off the edge of your work before returning. Never lift your rubber at the end of each stroke or turn it at the edge of the work. If you do this you will cause rubber marks on the work edges. Just keep your rubber working straight through your work, keeping the rubber as straight as possible in the path of each stroke. This final polishing of the surface is the most important part of the work. It is the final finish and if done correctly you will have a good, flat, clean and glossy finish which should also be completely free from any oil.

If you find that the work is dull when completed you may have used too much oil, which if not removed will result in a finish which will remain permanently dull, with no gloss showing at all. To obtain a good stiffed out finish you will need to practise and become familiar with using the rubber and applying polishes and oil. When stiffing out it is a good idea to use a clean rubber which is solely used for this purpose. Use a rubber made of a soft linen cover, which is not too hard but quite supple. Make sure the polish can flow quite freely when in use.

Another tip is to use polish which has been lightly thinned down with methylated spirits but take care not to soften the polished surface too much, otherwise the finished work may dull. A good product for this operation is known as 'finishing spirit', which can be purchased from some of the polish suppliers. It is very good for stiffing out and should be used carefully with a good clean rubber.

Spiriting out

For this process you need a well-made rubber of good quality linen. After completing the normal bodying up process you need a polish which is a half and half mixture of polish and methylated spirits. When the rubber is charged with this mixture you pass over the work surface area only once if your surface has been thoroughly bodied up so that you can just see that the polish has penetrated the surface. You then increase the pressure of your rubber and also use just a touch of linseed oil as your rubber becomes harder. However, you should find that your rubber will also become drier and at this stage you should stop using any more linseed oil.

With the drying rubber you will now be able to increase the pressure gradually – it is quite possible that you may need extra even pressure by using two hands on the rubber instead of one. Skilled polishers often adopt this procedure so that a good flat surface can be produced without any imperfections showing through. The finished surface should be very hard and clean with a fairly bright appearance.

You should now use the clear spiriting out method by simply using an old washed out polishing rubber which is lightly charged with methylated spirits. Always keep this rubber stored separately in a tin away from any other polishing rubbers. When using the rubber it may be safer to sprinkle a few drops of methylated spirit on its face and then lightly rub the face on the palm of the hand or the back of the hand to remove any excess 'wetness' of methylated spirit.

Now proceed to apply the face of the rubber to the work surface using light pressure with a brisk movement until the linseed oil smear completely disappears. You may increase the weight on the rubber as you proceed. If the smear of linseed oil is not completely removed you may have to repeat the process, but care must be taken not to use too

much, otherwise the finished work may dull. A wet a rubber, otherwise the methylated spirit burns and removes the polish instead of burnishing it. The technique is to use the rubber to burnish the polished surface with just the vapour of the methylated spirits. When the final finish is completed it may be necessary to rub lightly over the surface with a reviver to obtain a good clear gloss surface.

A further method of spiriting out is to use a good quality chamois leather for the cover of your rubber and apply a half-half mixture of methylated spirit and polish over the polished surface using light pressure with the rubber. Make sure you work in straight lines working left to right keeping even pressure at all times. The face of the chamois leather produces a good clean surface, allowing the polish and spirits to filter through; some people consider this method of spiriting superior to others.

The acid finish

Finally, a more sophisticated method of finishing a polished surface can be used. This is known as the 'acid finish' or 'vitriol finish' and is used to harden the surface of the polish. On completion of the bodying up process a final spiriting out can be done with a spirit rubber charged with a mixture of methylated spirits and gum benzoin. Take care not to use too much benzoin solution or you may burn the polished surface. The use of a little extra linseed oil will overcome any such problem. When using this rubber you will see the smear of oil working in over the surface and you should allow the rubber to work out quite dry.

At this stage you will have a fairly thin film of oil on the surface which needs to be removed before a gloss finish is ensured. To obtain a good clear gloss finish a mixture of water and sulphuric acid, mixed at 10:1 ratio, must be applied over the work surface simply by sprinkling it on with the fingers. This mixture is quite safe to use with your hands and will clean them as you use it.

After sprinkling the mixture over the work surface, using the ball of the palm of the hand, exert pressure with a firm steady motion over the work surface working to and fro away from you. It may be necessary to clean your hand using a drop of methylated spirit to clean off any dirt.

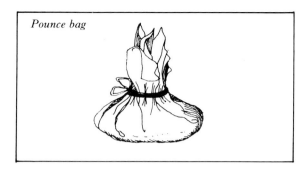

Pounce bag

When the smear of oil is nearly removed dust over the surface with Vienna chalk. The Vienna chalk can be applied from a pounce bag which is made from fine cotton cloth tied at the top. The pounce bag allows the fine chalk to filter through onto the work when lightly shaken over the work surface. Alternatively, the chalk can be dusted onto the hand, then rubbed over the work surface. After dusting the surface continue to burnish it with the ball of the palm of the hand, and as the chalk dries out, dust off the chalk with a clean dry rag, which should then bring the surface to a good clear, fine, glossy finish.

By using these materials to complete the acid finish, the weak acid solution will have killed the superfluous linseed oil used during the polishing process; finally the acid solution is also killed, absorbed and completely dried off by the Vienna chalk. It is possible to use a fine chamois leather instead of the ball of the palm of the hand to complete the burnishing operation, but this will depend on personal preference.

When using acid solutions such as sulphuric acid, you may have problems on the work surface. Marks could appear in the form of slight pitting or pock marks of chalk. If any of these problems arise it is safe to assume that your acid mixture is too strong, so therefore you should dilute your mixture with water. One other problem is that of colour change within the body of colour that would have been used during the bodying process. The acid may have had a bleaching action upon the coloured aniline dyes which may have been used. Always body up your work after you have stained and matched up the work. When mixing the acid solution, it is advisable to add the sulphuric acid to the water one drop at a time.

A good system for inexperienced polishers to adopt is to use the acid finish process when the final bodying up has been completed and before the spiriting out process. By using this method you should clear any marks or defects with the polish applied to the spirit rubber before attempting any final burnishing of the work surface with methylated spirits. Normally, if the final burnishing by the acid finish is done by a skilled polisher he will have completed his work using a few drops of ox-gall sprinkled on a piece of soft clean rag. This was used to act as a reviver. The modern method is to apply a proprietary reviver supplied by the polish manufacturer. Previously you could get ox-gall from the local butchers, which would be strained through crushed bone charcoal. The idea of using ox-gall was to prevent any finger-marks from appearing on the completed burnished surface.

This special acid finish is no doubt the best surface finish on French polish and was widely used for polishing pianos. Obviously, a great deal of skill and patience is required to obtain this high quality finish. However, if done properly the process is well worth the effort.

Glazing

The glazing of work was a quick, cheap and easy process for finishing off work which had been polished to a reasonable bodied finish; the pores of the wood must first be filled with polish though. This method can replace the spiriting out process but produces an inferior quality finish. Glaze is simply gum-benzoin which is crushed finely and dissolved in methylated spirits. After the mixture has been allowed to stand for a few hours it is then strained through fine nylon and bottled ready for use. The modern alternative is to use 'finishing spirit' which can be purchased at some polish suppliers.

Applying glaze

When applying glaze use a new rubber and keep it solely for glazing. Charge the rubber so that it is quite moist but not so wet that the glaze is likely to ooze out. Apply the glaze to the work surface by using the rubber in the direction of the grain. By doing this you will apply a wet glazed area following the path of the rubber. Always try to keep your rubber working in straight strokes in the direction of the grain, working over your work from left to right, end to end. Try to keep light, even pressure on the rubber that is, sufficient to make the glaze flow quite freely from your rubber giving you a wet surface area.

You may find that a few applications will be required to provide a satisfactory finish. You should apply your second coat when your first coat is dry. Allow up to five minutes for your first coat to dry and apply the second coat in exactly the same way. You should never attempt to apply glaze or finishing spirit in a circular motion otherwise you will leave circular rings on your work surface from the path of your rubber. Never apply glaze on a wet surface. Always allow the first coat of glaze to dry out before the second application, otherwise you may rough up the surface which could become contaminated with dust or small pieces of lint from the rubber.

Normally the glazing process is used for finishing all types of furniture which have narrow edges, such as chair rails, brackets, apron pieces, shelf edges, lattice work and any work which is really difficult to finish off with the spiriting out process.

'Tops' off polish

'Tops' or 'toppings' is another material used by the polisher for applying the final finish to work. It is said to be a more lasting quality finish than glaze. Application is by the same method as glazing. Tops is obtained by pouring the clear liquid polish off the top of white polish which has been allowed to settle in its container – hence the term tops or toppings. The only problem in using the tops off the white polish is that you reduce the strength of the polish; it is not, therefore, a good policy to adopt this method frequently. There is also no reason why you should not use a mixture of glaze and toppings together for some work. This mixture is ideal for use on less expensive work where the spiriting out process could be too expensive.

Dry shining

Where a quick, easy, smooth finish is required, especially on carcass interiors such as cabinets, wardrobes, drawers, interior shelvings and ply-wood sections the dry shine method is ideal. This is quick, easy to apply and quite cheap. The only materials required are thin polish, a polishing mop, a polishing rubber and some abrasive paper.

Depending on whether the timber is left natural or stained, you simply apply one coat of polish (colour of polish will depend upon your choice for colour matching) with the mop and allow to dry. Rub down the polish with fine garnet paper or lubrisil paper and apply a second coat of polish. Lightly rub down again and take a good clean rubber charged with polish and, working with the grain and with even pressure, work freely over the work surface to smooth it out. You will obtain a semi-gloss finish using this process. There is no grain filling with this process as the polish will sink into the pores of the wood and find its own level.

Aim to provide a good, clean, smooth, dry shine until a good semi-gloss appears with the minimum of effort. You are simply sealing the pores of the wood just to keep out any dirt or finger marks which would eventually show up on the wood if no protection were given. In the case of carcass work, shelves and drawers, these can be dry shined before fitting or gluing, which makes the work much easier to finish. On no account should you use any lubricant with your polish – no linseed oil. Always allow each coat of polish to dry before applying the next.

A moderate approach to dry shining is to apply a white shellac sanding sealer which incorporates a flatting agent to promote easy sanding. A quick application on top of this with a fairly wet rubber charged with polish will give you a good smooth finish. There are other much quicker-drying materials based on cellulose or synthetic lacquers which provide much harder and more water and chemical resistance than shellac-based materials. Some of these materials are toxic and, in some cases, require spray equipment to apply them.

Finally, there is no reason why a simple wax finish cannot be applied over the dry shine when the polish has finally dried out. The wax will give that little added protection.

Colouring

Commonly known as colour matching or just matching up is without doubt one of the most skilled operations in the finishing schedule of any polishing process. Ideally any furniture item should be made from timber cut from the same tree. This of course is not possible nowadays because timber is imported from various countries, grown in different conditions, having a range of colours when cut. Thus the polisher presented with different shades of timber must use his skills of colouring in order to provide an even shade of colour over the furniture item in question.

After completing the bodying in process and having partially choked up the grain with polish, your work should have settled down and no further sinking should take place. Then the colouring operation may begin. No matter what you intend to colour match, even if it is doors, drawers, legs, panels, tops or any other item, try to position your work in good light, preferably near a window. If you then stand back from your work you will see the areas that are considerably lighter, which must be colour matched. Never attempt to colour match any work which is in a poorly lit position.

A typical example of colour matching could be that of a chair made of mahogany where one leg is slightly lighter than the remaining three. To colour match the lighter leg you will need to mix some colour as follows: take a small container and mix one part polish with three or four parts methylated spirits together. Add a little aniline black (spirit black) and bismark brown (spirit red) to this mixture; you will then have a tinted spirit dye colour which will be warm brown, depending on the amount of dye added. (Only practice or trial and error can overcome the problems of colour mixing.) This mixture is then strained, if so desired, through an old nylon stocking or muslin. This straining will provide a good clear matching colour leaving no dye particles in the

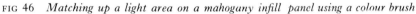

FIG 46 *Matching up a light area on a mahogany infill panel using a colour brush*

mixture. You then apply the colour to your chair leg using a good quality colour brush usually made of camel hair or squirrel hair.

Applying colour

Dip your colour brush into your container of spirit colour and remove the excess colour by lightly brushing the side of your brush on the edge of the container. The brush should be fairly moist with colour but not too wet. Now, starting at the top of the chair leg and working in the direction of the grain, apply the colour and work as quickly as possible so that you can overlap each application of colour, thus keeping a wet edge. Make sure you work round the leg from top to bottom so you have a fairly even colour match. It will be necessary to re-charge your brush from time to time during this operation so try to keep your brush moist at all times.

If any runs appear then you are applying your colour too thickly. Lightly wipe off the colour with methylated spirit and start again. The same method of applying colour applies to any part of furniture, whether it be a panel, chair rail, door style, chair runner or whatever. The essence of colouring is the speed of application and of course the mixing of the colour. It may be necessary to adjust your colour accordingly and of course you may need other spirit colours for this purpose such as spirit blue, spirit green, spirit yellow, spirit orange and so on.

Some polishers like to apply colour with a colour rubber instead of colour brush. This method of application requires the skill of using a rubber, and it would be better to try to colour flat surfaces first (small table tops) before attempting to colour chair frames or any carved types of furniture. When the colour has dried sufficiently, after about ten to twenty minutes, it may be necessary to apply a further application, depend-ing on whether you have matched up the colour correctly. If the colour match is correct, then you may proceed to 'fix' or 'fasten' the colour.

Fixing or fastening the colour

These terms fixing or fastening the colour simply mean that your choice is secured to the bodying up process by applying a coat of polish. Using a good quality polishing mop, apply a coat of polish using short swift strokes of the brush covering the whole work. Allow this coat of polish to dry for an hour or two to harden off. When dry you can proceed to body up the work and finish off by stiffing out, spiriting out or glazing. The main idea, of course, is to provide evenness of colour and if, at the early stage of staining, you can achieve this you will save a great deal of time at the colour matching stage. Colouring does require a great deal of skill and practice and any person who has a good eye for colour should obtain good results if he can master the art of application.

Blinding out

This operation consists of mixing polish, methy-lated spirits and pigment colours. Traditionally, especially in late Victorian and Edwardian per-iods, poor quality timber was often given a coat of blinding colour to obliterate the cheaper quality timbers, disfigurements in the timber, the sap-wood and so on. When you have achieved your background colour which may be oak, walnut or mahogany it is advisable to apply one coat of polish, which will just fix the blinding colour sufficiently so that you can now lightly paper down when the coat of polish is dry. At this stage, after papering down, the work would now be polished to the final finish using the appropriate coloured polish, button, garnet, orange, transpar-ent, etc. to produce the final desired coloured finish.

CHAPTER SIX

Finishing schedules

●

Knowing the full range of finishing materials available will enable you to choose a particular finishing schedule for any type of furniture item which requires re-finishing. In this chapter I shall attempt to deal with a complete range of finishing materials in selected schedules for certain types of timbers and furniture alike.

In the traditional polishing shop a polished surface is usually finished in one of two ways – close grained full finish or open grain finish. Various textured finishes may be obtained by matting, waxing or oiling together with certain decorative effects which could be any of the following: limed oak, weathered oak, bleaching, marbling, graining, fuming, ebonizing or enamelling. Decorative effects on timbers will be dealt with later so at this point I will deal with schedules for finishing various types of furniture.

Oak

Oak is a popular timber at the moment. By carefully selecting your materials you can produce a whole range of coloured finishes and with prac-

tice you may even come up with some special colours of your own. A little experiment could prove successful and very rewarding. Here are a few schedules for specific items which can be varied according to taste.

Oak chairs

The basic finishing schedule for all polishing work is usually as follows: stain; fill; seal; colour; coat in; body up; finish.

There are, however, variations on a theme and certain modifications arise owing to the particular job in question.

The following schedules are just a guide, together with a little information, some special features and suggestions for any modifications.

It is possible to purchase a good dark oil stain for this chair schedule, but if you find that the colour is too light add a little gas black to your stain and this will darken the timber further. Doing this, of course, will cause a certain amount of obliteration. Allow the stain to dry thoroughly

Schedule 1	**Jacobean oak**	
Application	*Material*	*Finish*
1 Stain	Jacobean oil stain	
2 Seal	Garnet polish	
3 Colour	Aniline dyes	Open grain gloss
4 Coat in	Garnet polish	
5 Body up	Garnet polish	
6 Finish	Finishing spirit	

Schedule 2	**Medium brown**	
Application	*Material*	*Finish*
1 Stain/fill	Filler stain	
2 Seal	Button polish	
3 Colour	Aniline dyes	Close grain, full finish gloss
4 Coat in	Button polish	
5 Body up	Button polish	
6 Finish	Pale polish	

Oak sideboards

Schedule 3	**Golden Oak**	
Application	*Material*	*Finish*
1 Stain	Bichromate of potash	
2 Oil Down	Linseed oil	
3 Filler	Light oak filler	
4 Seal	Orange polish	Close grain, full finish (high
5 Colour	Aniline dyes	gloss)
6 Coat in	Orange polish	
7 Body up (1)	Orange polish	
8 Body up (2)	Orange polish	
9 Finish	Spirit out with spirit rubber	

Schedule 4	**Natural oak**	
Application	*Material*	*Finish*
1 Seal	White polish or PVA	
2 Filler	Light grey filler	
3 Coat in	White polish or PVA	
4 Body up	White polish or PVA	Semi-close grain (gloss finish)
5 Colour	Aniline dyes	
6 Coat in	White polish or PVA	
7 Body up	White polish or PVA	
8 Finish	Stiff out with white polish	

Schedule 5	**Dark oak**	
Application	*Material*	*Finish*
1 Stain	Dark oak oil stain or dark oak water stain	
2 Filler	Dark oak oil bound	
3 Coat in	Garnet polish	Semi-close grain (gloss finish)
4 Body up	Garnet polish	
5 Colour	Aniline dyes	
6 Body up	Garnet polish	
7 Finish	Garnet polish	

Oak wall panelling

Schedule 6	**Warm brown oak**	
Application	*Material*	*Finish*
1 Stain	Warm brown oil stain or warm brown water stain or warm brown mixed solvent stain	
2 Coat in	Button polish	Open grain (gloss finish)
3 Body up	Button polish	
4 Colour	Aniline dyes	
5 Body up	Button polish	
6 Finish	Button polish	

and coat in with garnet polish. I have chosen this polish because of its colour: it adds a deep, rich golden tint to the Jacobean colour and really looks attractive, especially on English oak. Depending on how much polish you use in the bodying up process will determine your final colour. Finishing spirit produces the final gloss finish. If a much duller finish is required, then use a good quality matt wax which will reduce the gloss and subdue the colour. Any colouring would have been done after the sealing stage.

This schedule was very popular both before and after the Second World War and was often used on chairs which were made for restaurants, cafes and some schools. The use of a filler stain saves polish, produces added colour and at the same time helps to fill up the grain. Some chairs are left finished after button polish is applied, but this polish tends to be waxy and a final few rubbers of pale polish or even transparent polish help to stiffen up the surface finish. Usually the finish was left full gloss from the rubber.

For this particular colour we require good quality oak timber which should be heavily figured. When looking at the above schedule you will see that a chemical stain is used (bichromate of potash) which acts upon the tannic acid in the oak timber. This stain produces a deep, reddish yellow tone to the timber. After the stain has dried off, wipe over the surface with raw linseed oil. Lightly paper down after oiling. The oil acts as a lubricant whilst you paper and, of course, the raw linseed oil produces a deeper colour. At this stage you should apply a filler to which you can add a little yellow ochre to produce a yellow tint in the filler. The filler is applied in the normal way, and you should allow plenty of time for drying. Seal with orange polish using a rubber, working carefully in the direction of the grain. This finish, being costly to produce, requires a great deal of bodying up. This process will need to be repeated at least twice, if not more. It all depends on the depth of the oak grain after filling in. When the final bodying up is completed you may find the colour could be a little dead. If this is so, just add a little spirit red (bismark brown) to your polish, bodying up again, making sure to apply the polish evenly over the surface and then finish off. If you

do have to use the spirit red, take care – too much red will make the work too warm.

For the final finish you can 'stiff out' and then use the spiriting process for that high quality gloss finish.

The colour of natural oak timber will vary and probably require some colour matching during your schedule. The aim of producing natural oak is to preserve the natural whiteness of oak. Whatever material you may use to seal the oak will cause some form of yellowing. One of the best ways to overcome this yellowing problem is to apply a sealing coat of PVA (Polyvinyl acetate). This coating will help to preserve the natural colour to a certain degree, but, being a water based material, will obviously raise the grain of the timber.

To provide a uniformity of colour use a light grey pigmented filler. Unfortunately you will have partial obliteration of the grain. However, having previously sealed the timber with PVA obliteration should be minimal. The next stage is to coat in to fix the filler using either white polish or pva, body up with white polish, colour up with the aniline dyes if required, coat in again, and provide the final bodying up before finishing. The stiffing out process is considered to be adequate for this schedule. If you decide to use white polish throughout the schedule instead of PVA, there will be a very slight yellowing of your work. Remember, PVA is a milky white colour and should give you a much more natural oak colour.

If you decide not to have a gloss finish, then you may use a matting wax after the first bodying up stage. Make sure you do any colouring up before you coat in at stage three of the schedule. You will have less polish or PVA on your work, thus leaving the grain more open. This entails much less work, of course, and saves time.

Providing the oak timber is selected carefully, dark oak finishes can be very attractive. English oak lends itself ideally to a dark colour; when stained with a good dark oil stain the timber will look particularly attractive because of the nature of the grain.

The filler will add to the depth of colour and also save you much time in polishing. The use of garnet polish will give a nice deep rich tone to the finished colour. Any colouring can take place in stage five of the schedule or after coating in, in stage three. Remember to fix any colouring done with a coat of polish, otherwise you may wipe off the colour during your bodying up stage. The work can then be finished off with the simple stiffing up process.

This colour was often used on wall panelling in offices, shops, banks and the interiors of some fine country houses. The schedule is simple and easy to follow and the final result should be a rich warm brown oak colour. If, on the other hand, you require a much warmer colour, then orange polish can be substituted for the button polish. No filler is used so the colour is derived from the stain and polish only. Any colouring will be achieved by mixing weak solutions of the aniline black and reds. Sometimes a little weak brown umber or orange chrome may be needed for blinding out unwanted colours, such as black marks in the oak timber. Complete the work by bodying up with button polish and simply stiff out the work.

This was a very popular finish for showcase work as well as wall panelling in the 1930s. Many of the now demolished old cinemas had walls panelled in oak, which was polished to a light oak colour. Sometimes the timber would have been bleached because certain oak panels were much darker and required lightening before the filler application. This schedule is relatively simple to follow and looks crisp and clean when the work is completed. If you need to use any pigment colours for blinding out or matching up purposes, use yellow ochre, flake white or titanium white. You will only require small amounts for tinting purposes. Watch the titanium white — it is a very strong white and only a little is needed. Mix the pigments in white polish and use sparingly. For final finishing use the stiffing out process.

This schedule was often used on selected quartered oak and looked excellent when finished. Unfortunately, on ageing the colour tends to darken and attract dirt in the grain.

Walnut

A timber which is scarce, expensive and not very popular currently. Of course English walnut is the most well-known but there are others, such as American black walnut and Indian walnut. Personally, I think this timber is one of the best for the woodfinisher to practise his skills on. Walnut lends itself to numerous colours, both warm and cold, dark and light. The timber was extensively used for veneers on cabinet work, pianos and bedroom suites and for solid show wood on chair frames from the mid-nineteenth century up to the 1930s.

Schedule 7	Light oak	
Application	Material	Finish
1 Filler	Light oak filler	
2 Coat in	White polish	
3 Colour	Pigment colours	
4 Body up	White polish	Semi-close grain (gloss finish)
5 Finish	White polish	

Tables

Schedule 8	Medium walnut	
Application	Material	Finish
1 Stain	Vandyke brown water stain or medium brown oil stain	
2 Filler	Walnut filler	
3 Coat in	Button or orange polish	
4 Colour	Aniline dyes	
5 Body up	Button or orange polish	Full grain (high gloss)
6 Coat in	Button or orange polish	
7 Body up	Button or orange polish	
8 Finish	Finishing spirit	

Here are some finishing schedules which would be suitable for walnut.

If you used English walnut you might well come across sapwood, which is very light in colour and requires staining to match up to the remainder of the timber. This could be done with water stain, by mixing the shade accordingly and applying slightly on the light side. A mixture of spirit black and bismark brown (aniline dyes) could also be used for this purpose, but take care with the bismark brown if this stain is chosen as it is a strong red. If you use water stains, remember they will raise the grain slightly. Walnut oil stain would overcome this problem.

Apply the filler when the stain is completely dry, ensuring that you remove all the excess filler properly. Allow the filler to stand for at least four hours so that no finishing problems arise in the latter stages of finishing. Any colouring should be done between the coating in stage and the bodying up stage. Take care when colouring, otherwise you may obliterate the natural walnut grain. Great skill is required when matching up walnut owing to the heavily figured grain.

When the final bodying up process has been completed use a little pale or transparent polish to give that extra gloss finish. You can use finishing spirit for this. For a high quality finish it is better to stiff out than spirit out.

You will find that a great deal of American whitewood (canary wood) was used for faking walnut around the 1930s. The procedure was to stain first, then grain and finally polish. The timber was used on the cheaper types of furniture.

FIG 47 *Polishing a walnut carving with a rubber*

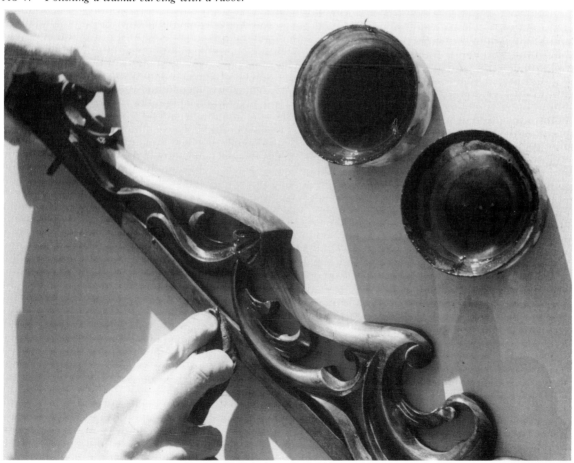

This particular schedule is ideal for polishing Italian walnut, some of which has a dark, heavily figured grain and when polished with garnet polish tends to produce a deep rich brown golden colour. Careful selection of the stain is required; don't use a stain which is too red. Choose a more brown walnut stain or even a cold walnut stain with a hint of gold tint in its colour. Use a good quality oil-bound woodfiller or thixotropic (one that becomes temporarily liquid when shaken and is otherwise gel-like) filler to fill in the grain. If you require extra clarity of final colour then seal the stain first with a thin coat of garnet polish and then apply the woodfiller on top of the sealer coat.

Follow the remainder of the schedule using garnet polish, colour up if necessary and in the final stages use pale polish to obtain the high gloss finish. Stiff out or spirit out as desired.

No doubt you can see that this finishing schedule is somewhat lengthy and will, of course, be costly to produce at today's labour charges. It is not uncommon for one well-known establishment in the West End of London to quote over £1000 for polishing a piano. This finish is no doubt the 'Rolls Royce' of polishing and if executed properly it is hard to distinguish between a hand-finished piano and a spray-finished piano.

Concerning the actual schedule, it is worth noting that there are extra bodying up stages in the schedule, these being necessary to enable the high build film thickness to be achieved. The choice of polish will depend on the colour required. The final finish would be a transparent finish or a special pale polish finish which would produce a gloss effect, and then to obtain clarity of finish a good quality reviver could be used to produce brilliance.

When adopting this schedule allow adequate drying time between each bodying up stage to enable solvent evaporation to take place, thus allowing sinkage.

To obtain this special piano finish we must adopt the 'acid finish' process described in Chapter 5. The acid finish process is uneconomical at today's costs but if a customer can really afford this class of finish, I am sure that he will be well satisfied with the results. The general appearance of figure in English walnut is quite exceptional.

This is a simple schedule which relies on the linseed oil for colour together with the garnet polish which will produce that dark golden tint. If a much warmer colour is required then a red oil can be used instead of the linseed oil. Again, the

FIG 48 *Touching in a light patch on walnut veneer with a pencil brush*

FIG 49 *Applying polish with a mop*

choice of colour will depend on one's own preference. Take care to allow the oil to dry out sufficiently before polishing, otherwise sweating may occur, thus causing problems during the later stages of polishing. The final finish can be stiffed out or spirited out as desired.

This is a very common colour for traditional walnut finishes. It was often used on showcases and display cabinets and is a very rich bright colour tending to be on the very warm side. The beauty of walnut is its grain texture, and therefore using oil stains, water stains or simply just linseed

Schedule 9	**Golden walnut**	
Application	*Material*	*Finish*
1 Stain	Walnut oil stain	
2 Filler	Walnut oil bound filler	
3 Coat in	Garnet polish	
4 Colour	Aniline dyes	Full grain (high gloss)
5 Body up	Garnet polish	
6 Coat in	Garnet polish	
7 Body up	Garnet polish	
8 Finish	Pale polish	

Pianos
Schedule 10

Application	*Material*	*Finish*
1 Stain	Walnut oil stain	
2 Filler	Walnut woodfiller	
3 Coat in	Button, orange or garnet	
4 Colour	Aniline dyes	
5 Body up a	Use polish of	High build, full gloss,
6 Body up b	your own choice	burnish
7 Body up c	from button, orange or garnet	
8 Finish	Special pale polish	
9 Burnish	Acid and Vienna chalk	
10 Reviver	Proprietary reviver	

Clock cases
Schedule 11 **Dark golden walnut**

Application	*Material*	*Finish*
1 Oil	Linseed oil	
2 Coat in	Garnet polish	
3 Colour	Aniline dyes	Semi-full grain
4 Body up a	Garnet polish	High gloss
5 Body up b	Garnet polish	
6 Finish	Special pale polish	

Showcases and display cabinets
Schedule 12 **Brown walnut**

Application	*Material*	*Finish*
1 Stain	Brown walnut water stain	
2 Filler	Warm walnut filler	
3 Coat in	Button or orange polish	
4 Colour	Aniline dyes	Full grain gloss
5 Body up a	Button or orange polish	
6 Body up b	Button or orange polish	
7 Finish	Transparent	

oil enhances it. However, in this instance we rely on a water stain with the addition of one of the warmer polishes – button or orange. Whichever polish you choose, finish off with a few rubbers of transparent polish just to give you that extra gloss.

Mahogany

Like walnut, mahogany is an expensive timber and very attractive when polished, especially the 'feather' mahogany veneers. Because mahogany timbers are warm red in colour, they accept red oil stains, warm water stains and of course red oils. However, the tendency today (in modern finishing that is) is to use too much tinting colour, which simply obliterates the grain and thus removes the clarity of the grain texture). Just because mahogany is a warm timber it does not mean that it was polished in nothing but warm red colours. In fact, there are brown, golden and at one time even bleached mahoganies. It all depends on taste and the colour fashion of the period.

One of the fashion colours of the 1920s and 30s was a colour known as chippendale mahogany. This is a very dark reddish-brown mahogany which started off as a *deep* reddish-brown and, of course, faded with age. One of the most popular pieces of cabinet work to be polished in this colour

FIG 50   *Coating a turned rail with button polish*

was the upright piano. (See Schedule 15)

Another type of furniture which was in fashion at the turn of the century was the Louis-type cabinet. These were polished almost black, and the aniline black and bismark browns were used to obtain the deep damson red-black mahogany colour. Here are schedules for different colours you could use.

In using the schedule you can produce a similar colour to the old chippendale mahogany colour of the turn of the century and, of course, the colour will fade with time and mellow down to a colour similar to the original chippendale. By applying the bichromate of potash water stain you achieve the deep reddish-brown colour common to this type of furniture of the period, and by polishing with a slightly red tinted button polish during the final bodying process, added warmth will be given to the overall colour. Finish off with button polish to give added protection to the colour.

A common enough colour used for pianos in the early part of the century, it requires a really simple schedule. Instead of the slower drying oil-bound fillers you can use the quicker drying thixotropic filler to save time. If you do so, remember to work quickly with it and apply the filler in small areas. Make sure you remove *all* the surplus filler. Button polish will give you the warmth in the colour without making it too red. If you need to use any colour, make sure you use it early in the schedule, preferably soon after you have applied your first coat of button polish or at least soon after a few rubbers of polish. The work can be completed by stiffing out, then spiriting out.

This colour was sometimes known as damson or plum in the piano trade and is an attractive finish. However, owing to the great amount of spirit dye, coloured filler and tinted polish used, the grain will be somewhat obliterated and the general characteristic of the finished colour will be opaque. Very few pianos seem to be polished in this way today, the colour was once fashionable but now not to everyone's liking. Great skill is needed in applying the stain evenly; you must apply the polish correctly, making sure that you apply an even amount of tinted polish over each part of the piano carcass, otherwise the various parts will take on an uneven effect and will need re-matching. Again, any colouring must be done as early as possible so that the bulk of the colour is buried well under the tinted polish. All the work should be matched up evenly before any final finishing is attempted. To produce that extra special gloss, use transparent polish and spirit out your work. Polishers used to use a velvet or chamois leather over the wadding when final finishing on piano work – used skilfully, the results were quite exceptional.

This is probably one of the most popular

Cabinet work

Schedule 13   Chippendale mahogany

Application	Material	Finish
1 Stain	Bichromate of potash	
2 Filler	Dark mahogany oil bound	
3 Coat in	Button polish	
4 Colour	Aniline dyes	Full grain gloss
5 Body up a	Button polish	
6 Body up b	Tinted red button polish	
7 Finish	Button polish	

Mahogany pianos (1)

Schedule 14   Warm brown mahogany

Application	Material	Finish
1 Stain	Red mahogany oil stain	
2 Filler	Mahogany oil bound	
3 Coat in	Button polish	Full grain
4 Colour	Aniline dyes	High gloss
5 Body up a	Button polish	
6 Body up b	Button polish	
7 Finish	Transparent polish	

Mahogany pianos (2)

Schedule 15   Red plum mahogany

Application	Material	Finish
1 Stain	Spirit maroon or purple	
2 Filler	Warm mahogany (rose pink)	
3 Coat in	Tinted red polish	
4 Colour	Aniline dyes	Full grain high gloss
5 Body up a	Tinted red polish	
6 Body up b	Tinted red polish	
7 Finish	Transparent polish	

Mahogany pianos (3)

Schedule 16   Black polish

Application	Material	Finish
1 Stain	Spirit black or gas black	
2 Filler	Black oil bound	
3 Coat in	Black polish	
4 Colour	Aniline black	High build full gloss burnish
5 Body up a		
6 Body up b	Black polish	
7 Body up c		
8 Finish	Transparent polish	
9 Burnish	Acid and Vienna chalk	
10 Reviver	Proprietary reviver	

finishes for pianos, especially for the concert grand pianos and sometimes known as the 'German finish'. This is because nearly all the German baby grand and concert grand pianos were polished black. The only problem with this colour is its tendency to show distinct marks which are sometimes difficult to remove. Again, great skill is required when applying the colours because there are various shades of black and you must always use the same blacks throughout the job. Gas black does provide a much deeper black in some respects, but if you do decide to use this

Cabinet work and chairs

Schedule 17   Sheraton mahogany

Application	Material	Finish
1 Stain	Bichromate of potash	
2 Filler	Mahogany	
3 Coat in	Orange polish	
4 Colour	Aniline colours	
5 Body up a		High build full gloss
6 Body up b	Orange polish	
7 Body up c		
8 Finish 1	Tinted orange with bismark brown	
9 Finish 2	Spirit out with spirit rubber containing about 70% to 80% spirit	

Shopfittings (interiors)

Schedule 18   Red mahogany

Application	Material	Finish
1 Stain	Oil stain or ngr stain	
2 Filler	Mahogany thixotropic	
3 Coat in	Button polish	
4 Colour	Aniline dyes	High build full gloss
5 Body up a	Button polish	
6 Body up b	Button polish	
7 Finish	Transparent polish	

Shopfittings (exteriors)

Schedule 19   Warm brown mahogany

Application	Material	Finish
1 Stain	Mahogany oil stain	
2 Filler	Mahogany thixotropic	
3 Coat in	Button polish	High build gloss
4 Colour	Aniline dyes	
5 Body up a	Button polish	
6 Body up b	Button polish	
7 Finish	Oil varnish	

Wall panelling

Schedule 20   Bleached mahogany

Application	Material	Finish
1 Bleach	Apply A solution	
2 Bleach	Apply B solution	
3 Neutralise	Cold water	
4 Coat in	White polish	Gloss finish
5 Body up a	White polish	
6 Body up b	White polish	
7 Finish	Transparent polish	

black make sure you strain the polish well if *mixing yourself*. Do not mix spirit black and gas black together. Make up your mind which one to use and stay with it.

Considerable patience is needed for polishing; allow each bodying up process to dry sufficiently before proceeding to the next. Traditionally one or two pianos were polished at the same time, changing from one to the other, to allow adequate drying of each piano part. The final finish must be absolutely flat and glossy before any attempt is made to use the burnishing process. The acid and chalk finish will provide you with that brilliant piano finish for which the concert grand pianos were renowned.

A very high class finish on mahogany timbers which really looks good on mahogany curl, fiddle back and feather mahoganies. By using bichromate of potash you get a deep rich red mahogany colour that brings out the special grains mentioned. An alternative to using the chemical stain is to use a red oil or linseed oil. These oils were sometimes used on the Spanish mahoganies that really did not need staining. The use of oil produced the deep colour of these mahoganies.

If you decide to use the bichrome stain, it is a good idea to use an orange polish to give you that nice warm mahogany colour which isn't too red. Sometimes if too strong a red stain is used the work can be very fiery. On the other hand, if you require the work to be much warmer, then the introduction of a little bismark brown to your finishing orange polish will suffice. Be careful, however – too much red can be disastrous. For that brilliant gloss it is better to spirit out your work with a clean spirit rubber.

This is a common schedule for shopfitting interiors, which looks extremely good when finished. Nowadays you can use the quicker drying thixotropic fillers instead of the old slow drying oil bound fillers. Button polish will give you the warm brown mahogany colour without being too red. If you require a less warm mahogany colour you should stain your work with a brown mahogany stain in place of the normal red mahogany stain. Complete your work by bodying up twice with a good quality button polish and finish off with a few rubbers of transparent polish, using the stiffing out method.

A traditional finish for exterior shopfittings, which gives good protection and is reasonable to maintain. The work is usually washed down and re-varnished from time to time without you having to strip off the original finish. One way of

FIG 51 *Applying spirit black on a chair leg using a mop*

FIG 52 *Coating a chair leg with black polish*

69

FIG 53 *Applying bleach to a chairframe*

FIG 54 *Scrubbing the chairframe with water to neutralize the bleach*

speeding up the schedule is to use a stain or filler and apply both together in one operation. The traditional oil-based varnish is applied to protect the button polish, this being the final finish.

This is a finishing schedule that is popular on selected figured mahoganies, including mahogany curl, fiddle back and feather. The bleaching agents used are sodium hydroxide (the A solution) and hydrogen peroxide (the B solution). Plenty of cold water should be used to wash out the bleach-ing chemicals before any white polish is applied. The white polish will keep the colour light and clean but it does tend to dry slowly and is not a hard finish. A few rubbers of transparent polish provide the final gloss finish.

Bleached mahogany was popular on some cabinet furniture 50 years ago and also on ship furniture and panelling. Some specialist shops were also fitted out with bleached wall panelling, including jewellers, clothes shops and restaurants.

CHAPTER SEVEN

Finishing faults and remedies

●

When French polishing you will often come across some undesirable fault; there are many possible defects, some due to bad workmanship and others due to some particular contaminant, for example, water or alkali. Other problems arise from different grades of polish being used on one particular project and some from the use of stains, woodfillers, bleaches and oils. Whatever the problems, they must be rectified, and each material used in the finishing schedule must be identified correctly in every detail. Thus an accurate assessment can be made of each material used in the schedule, the method of application and the preparation of each material.

Most finishing faults are due to faulty materials, faulty application, poor preparation of the timber or veneers, bad working conditions or possibly a combination of all four. A good point worth noting is to try to reproduce the unwanted effect with all the relevant factors under control. If the fault persists, however, then the material itself should be investigated. It must be pointed out that an unknown factor which could be temporary, could cause the fault. Some of the faults which are very difficult to trace are those which unfortunately keep re-appearing. Some of the more common faults which can usually be overcome are as follows.

Chilling
This is one of several problems related to atmosphere; it appears on the polished surface when you apply polish. Chilling usually shows itself by a milky white appearance on the polished surface which is due to fast drying solvents evaporating from the polish film and also to a drop in temperature in the workshop. If conditions of humidity arise a fall in temperature can also cause precipitation of moisture from the air. This moisture works as a non-solvent for the solids and usually precipitates the shellac resin. The remedy for this particular finishing fault is simply to increase the workshop temperature.

Crazing
This 'cracking' of the polished surface is one of the more common problems in woodfinishing. The most common factor in crazing is that in whatever form it shows itself, it will be due to surface tensions within the polish film. Probably the most common cause is the use of a hard polish over a soft one or a fast polish over a slow-drying polish. When French polishing use the same type of polish throughout the whole finishing schedule.

When French polish is applied to a timber surface, owing to its sticky consistency, linseed oil is also added separately and it is this material which can also cause crazing if used indiscriminately. The linseed oil will polymerize within the polish film and will also provide a fair amount of non-reversibility. However, if the oil is used in excess it will cause crazing as polymerizing continues when the shellac resin has dried and the solvent has evaporated.

Traditionally, when re-polishing old furniture, polishers sometimes used soda and water to clean off the old dirt and grime from the polished surface. If too much soda was used it attacked the old polished surface, which then began to perish. Obviously, if you intend to re-polish on a soda-washed surface you should make sure that all the soda water is washed off completely.

Another problem which arose quite frequently was the cracking of a polished surface on a piano case. Pianos were often finished with the acid and chalk process and this process produced a very hard surface. If a new surface is to be applied over this hard film it is necessary to flatten down the cracked surface to attempt to eliminate the cracks in the film. One way of doing this is to use pumice powder and water or pumice powder and thin linseed oil. Remove all the water or oil, and when the surface is completely dry you can re-polish. Soften the old polished surface with a few rubbers of weak polish or alternatively a thin coat of polish by brush. By doing this you will provide a softer surface to work on, more elasticity and hopefully a more homogeneous surface.

If the cracked or crazed surface is very bad, however, no amount of flattening will improve that surface. You will need to remove the old polish completely: strip off the surface with stripper, neutralize with solvent and re-finish with one of the finishing schedules mentioned in the previous chapter.

Fading

This problem usually arises, not from poor workmanship, but from possible exposure to sunlight or dampness. A faded polished surface will require re-finishing and a finishing system will need to be adopted. Firstly, a faded surface will have dull colour with little or no shine at all. To improve this lightly remove the top layer of polish with fine abrasive paper, say flour paper or 400 grade silicon carbide paper. After you have used the chosen abrasive, clean off the surface and apply a few rubbers of polish to provide a key for the next operation. Then apply a new layer of colour to bring the work back to its original colour. By using your aniline dyes and a little polish for binding, mix the colour as near as possible to the original shade and then apply this to the faded area. If the colour is not accurate do not worry—you can use a coloured polish to get the colour nearer to its original shade.

You may find that the old chippendale and sheraton mahogany colours tend to fade and they need to be re-coloured and polished. Of course to avoid the fading of a polished surface keep your furniture away from strong sunlight and also damp areas.

Flaking

Normally flaking is caused by lack of adhesion. Some of the causes are using oil stains that have too much bitumen content or using some wood-fillers that are too oily. Other problems also arise, including poor adhesion on some repairs when re-finishing. Poor interface adhesion is a common problem. Also, films age, and some polishes progressively become brittle due to loss of moisture.

In varnishing, the top surface sometimes lifts off from the ground coat. Although this is rare, it could be caused by the ground coat being too greasy or even too hard, thus not giving good interface adhesion. Other causes of flaking on varnishes could be moisture in the timber, poor quality varnishes or even bad pigments in the early use of base colours.

There is no remedy for flaking surface coatings caused by the film disintegrating. The only solution is to remove the bad area, re-colour and then re-finish with good quality materials, making sure that the fault does not recur. Obviously, good preparation of timber and materials is the ideal answer to avoid this unsightly problem. Sometimes it may mean that the whole work will need to be stripped and re-finished, such is the damage caused by the contaminants mentioned previously.

Greasy surface

A greasy surface is usually only seen after the work is finished and sometimes does not become evident until after a few hours or days afterwards. If this occurs you have used too much oil when applying your polish. Use a rag to remove it which has been damped with white spirit and wipe over the oily surface. Dry off with a clean rag. It will

1 **A** Fumed oak
B Fumed oak with a coating of matt wax

2 Button shellac

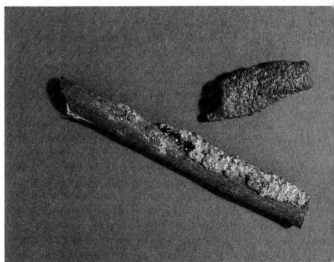

3 Stick lac on twig

4 Weathered oak

5 Red brown oak with limed finish

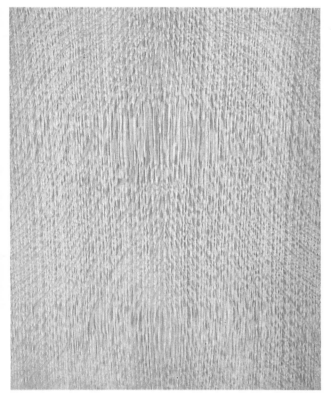

6 Limed oak

7 Utile mahogany with oil varnish finish

8 **A** Dark golden walnut (gloss finish)
  B Golden walnut (gloss finish)

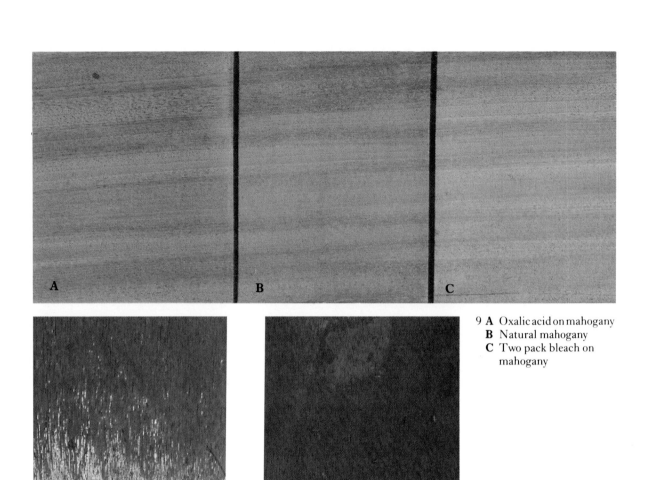

A   B   C

9 **A** Oxalic acid on mahogany
  B Natural mahogany
  C Two pack bleach on
     mahogany

10   Woodfiller faults
  A Polishing on wet filler
     (white in the grain)
  B Insufficient removal of filler
  C Clean filled surface
  D Slight obliteration of grain

11 Types of resin
A Dammar Batu
B Kauri
C Capal
D Dammar Pale

12 Types of Wax
A Beeswax
B Canauba
C Japan
D Paraffin

13   Gloss finishes on oak timber   **C** Light oak
    A Dark oak   **D** Golden oak
    B Warm brown oak

14   Timbers   **C** Satinwood
    A Beech   **D** Yew
    B Elm

15 Timbers
  A Rio rosewood
  B Chestnut
  C Sycamore
  D Makore

16 Examples of graining
  A Rosewood
  B Warm walnut

17 Examples of scumbling
  A Black
  B Red
  C Yellow

18 Mahogany finishing schedule
  A Mahogany timber
  B Brown oil stain
  C Dark mahogany woodfiller
  D Coat of button polish
  E Body up and finish with button polish

now be necessary to re-polish the surface but this time use less oil.

Gritty surface

This is possibly caused by using varnishes that are too cold, possibly chilled, damp or have been stored in frosty conditions. The actual manufacture of the varnish could be faulty, or you could be using dirty brushes. To avoid these problems always use good quality varnish brushes which are clean, work in clean conditions and try to apply varnishes in conditions which are conducive to good work. In practice, it is practically impossible to avoid some form of dust contamination, but you can help the situation in some cases by putting water on the ground to avoid rising dust and also to use tac-rags to wipe over the surface before applying your varnish.

Muddiness

Muddiness is a problem which is usually related to woodfillers. During formulation sometimes there is too much emphasis on the colouring agent, pigments which cause an obliterating effect. Consequently, when these colours are incorporated in the formulation of woodfillers the pigments which are used are left on the surface of the timber as well as in the pores of the grain and therefore tend to cause this muddy appearance under the polish.

One other cause is really in woodfiller formulation. With manufacturers producing faster drying woodfillers sometimes there is insufficient binding agent used in the mix; this tends to leave the pigments on the surface of the wood, causing an opaque appearance. It is wise to choose woodfillers carefully and use the types which provide good, clear colours.

Introducing a little binding agent can overcome opaque pigment problems in the faster drying woodfillers. Add about ten per cent binding agent to the mix. Allow adequate drying time for this filler if you adopt this procedure.

Dull varnish

When varnish loses its shine it can be simply revived. Mix up equal parts of linseed oil, vinegar and turpentine and rub the mixture over the surface, polishing off with a good quality chamois leather. Finally polish with a lint-free cloth just to provide that final finish. The chamois leather burnishes the varnish really well and gives a good shine. The reviving mixture is compatible with the oil-bound type varnishes so no further problem should arise.

Puffiness

This occurs when the filler lacks adequate binding agent and consequently accepts more solvent. The filler then swells within the grain and the polish hardens over this swelling, thus showing a grain pattern over the surface. To overcome this fault flatten down the surface; you will have to re-polish it because the filler will tend to sink after the solvent has dried out of the filler.

Pitting or cissing

In varnish work this problem takes the form of small holes on the varnish surface sometimes known as a 'ciss'. This is usually caused by some foreign body, which could be grease, dirt or a silicone contaminant. These foreign bodies cause surface tensions and repel any wet varnish. They can also be caused by too much turpentine being used in the varnish or over-varnishing where there is too much moisture in the atmosphere. Never use a varnish brush which has been recently washed out in turpentine. Always allow drying of washed out brushes before use. To eliminate pitting marks you should flat down the surface and re-varnish.

Ropiness (varnish)

This is due to poor storage of varnish products. It is essential to attempt to store varnishes in a constant temperature. Normally, if a varnish is stored in a cold place the material tends to thicken up and when it is applied to a surface it becomes ropy, thus showing long streaks. Never bring out cold varnish into a warm workshop and use it immediately. Allow the varnish to acclimatize before use. Sometimes old varnishes are more susceptible so it is advisable to check old stock before using it on the work in question. Always make sure your varnish is mixed well and at ambient temperature before use.

Ropiness (polish)

This is a fault caused by poor polishing. You may not be using the polishing rubber correctly: if the polished surface tends to show up ridges along the direction of the grain you are probably not using the polishing figure of eight pattern the circular motion or the oval pattern enough. You could also be using a cloth on your rubber which is very coarsely woven or too fine, thus causing these ridges. You may be using polish which is too thin or too oily. This excess of oil also causes a ropy effect if you polish along the grain too frequently.

If the ropy effect is not too serious, then a good flattening down with turpentine and linseed and a medium grade abrasive paper is sufficient. Make sure that the polish is hard, however, before you attempt any flattening, otherwise you could rip out the polish.

Streaks in the varnish

This is a problem which could arise from the varnish by poor mixing of driers, oils and turpentines within the varnish formulation. If this fault appears on the surface usually a light rubbing down, when dry, and a further coat of good quality varnish will overcome it.

Sweating

Sweating occurs quite often with new polishers, trainees, apprentices and students when they use too much oil in the polishing process. Unfortunately the problem cannot be solved quickly because the oil forces its way through the polish after standing for some time and can take weeks, if not months, to clear. A good quality reviver will help to remove the oil or, if that fails to do the trick, use a mild detergent, flat down with pumice powder and then re-polish the whole work.

Sweating can also be caused by poor quality polish or spirits. Some polishes are greasy and, when used with oil, the polished surface also becomes greasy in texture. Try to use best quality materials at all times, and the problems of sweating should be avoided. Polishing your work with just the correct amount of oil for lubrication is something learned only with practice.

White-in-the-grain

This fault is common to solvents used in the formulation of woodfillers. The solvent becomes trapped under the polish and being a non-solvent for the polish tends to precipitate through the film. With the thixotropic-type fillers this fault

FIG 55 *An example of a ropy finish on a polished surface (ropiness)*

FIG 56 *A white ring mark on a polished surface*

should not show itself because they dry fairly fast. Of course you should always allow your fillers to dry out properly before applying any polish, thus avoiding trapping any solvents which are incompatible with the polish.

White ring marks
This is a fault which is usually caused by heat or moisture, or both combined which appears on the surface of French polish. The heat tends to expand the polish surface thus allowing the moisture to penetrate the film surface which then causes precipitation. The problem can be further intensified by hot vessels placed on the polished surface. Obviously you should always protect a polished surface from any hot plate by using a place mat.

However, to remedy this fault sometimes a mild rubbing with oil will be sufficient. If not, use a swab of wadding soaked in methylated spirits, wipe over the white mark with the spirits and set alight with a match or taper. Blow out the flame before it has completely burnt out. it may be necessary to repeat this operation two or three times depending on the severity of the mark. The surface will probably appear dull after burning so restore it with a few rubbers of polish. If there are no dull areas after burning out then a good reviving is probably all that is required.

One point which is worth noting is the safety factor in relation to burning out. Keep any oils, spirits, wadding and any other flammable materials well away from your lighted matches or tapers. This practice is a trick of the trade and

FIG 57 *Water and scratch marks on a gateleg table*

should be undertaken with great care, with safety in mind.

Water marks

This is a very common fault on polished surfaces where flower vases have been allowed to stand on tables, sideboards, etc. Spilled water that has been left for considerable time penetrates the polish, causing an unsightly water mark. Sometimes the mark can be removed by a simple wipe over with camphorated oil, which must be well rubbed into the polish. Wipe off the excess oil and then re-polish the surface. If severe, the water mark could also be burned out in a similar way to white ring marks.

Surface scratches

Scratches on a polished surface are a very common problem. It is not always easy to remove a scratch and it calls for a great deal of skill. How the polisher treats the scratch will depend upon the nature of the damage. Normally, a surface scratch will only require the top layer or so of polish to be removed so that the depth of the scratch can be reached. However, in some instances the scratch will be so deep that it penetrates the wood and therefore most of the polish will need to be removed; the scratch will require filling with a suitable stopper, matched up to the existing colour and re-polished.

To remove the top layer of polish you can lightly sand down the polished surface or use a cabinet scraper, then sand down. Alternatively, rub over with a rag damped with methylated spirit to partially remove the polish. The most difficult scratches to remove are those which show diagonally across the grain. Because of the nature of the grain structure it is very difficult to remove this type of scratch completely. One way of achieving a satisfactory result is to remove the polish around the scratched area, fill in the scratch with the correct matching stopper and then match up the surrounding area with the required colours. These could be aniline dyes or pigments or a combination of the two. Finally, re-polish the damaged area. It may, however, be necessary to re-polish the whole area of the work to produce a satisfactory job.

There are much quicker ways of touching up scratches with patent scratch removers and various other methods but the best way is to attempt to eliminate the scratch completely and re-polish, especially if the work is a good quality piece of furniture or an antique. Sometimes in the long term it can be much cheaper to re-polish the whole surface after repairing the scratch rather than concentrating on one particular damaged area.

CHAPTER EIGHT

Varnishes and varnishing

●

Types of varnish

Although French polish was a very popular surface coating during the last century we must not forget another transparent coating – oleoresinous varnish. Varnish is very flexible and its durability is more important to the use of exterior surface coatings. We must remember that French polish is an attractive finish, giving good colour and texture, but that it has no resistance to the outside elements. We must therefore look to other materials for external use and of course we usually consider transparent varnish coatings for the extra protection required.

Varnishes can be produced as a matt finish or gloss finish. However, we must turn to other methods of application concerning these materials, namely varnish mops and brushes. We cannot use the rubber method used in French polishing because the oil based varnishes tend to be resinous and slow drying and would cause problems with the rubber.

Oleoresinous varnishes

Generally there are three main groups of varnishes, as follows: (a) a two-can isocyanate polyurethane; (b) a one-can moisture absorbing polymer; and (c) a one-can urethane oil oxidizing type. The first type (a) is a fully cross-linked polymer which dries very fast and is very hard when fully cured. The second (b) is similar to the first but requires the addition of moisture to achieve full maturity. Finally, the third type (c) is really only an up-graded resin varnish.

From experience I would choose the second type of varnish because of its reasonable drying time and ease of application. You may find that the oxidizing oil-type varnish is much easier to apply, but its life is limited owing to its poorer weathering properties.

Whatever type of varnish you decide to use, it is paramount that the substrate is carefully prepared before any varnish coating is applied. You should aim for a good film thickness for maximum protection; this could be as many as three or four coats of varnish in order to prevent any breakdown of the film.

Water-based varnishes

There are other varnishes, however, which are not so common today: water-based and spirit-based types. These two varnishes dry by solvent evaporation, water-based varnishes being particularly popular for protecting paper. Some shellac resins were used in conjunction with the water-based formulations but required an adjustment in the formulation because shellac resins are incompatible with water. A boric acid solution was required, commonly known as borax.

Spirit-based varnishes

Some of the traditional spirit varnishes were the shellac-based, white and brown hard varnishes, Japan varnish, flat varnish, paper varnish and of course the knotting varnish used by decorators. You may come across some of the old furniture which was commonly coated with a spirit varnish

– such as kitchen chairs, tables, food cupboards, old hand rails and, of course, the shopfront. Probably the most common use of a varnish was in floor finishing. The varnish would be a varnish stain type with added colour in various shades of mahogany, oak or pine. These varnishes are now manufactured with the amateur in mind and, of course, they are for brush application only.

Because spirit varnishes dry by solvent evaporation and are shellac-based, they are like French polish. However, because varnish is more viscous it cannot be applied with a polishing rubber. Generally a varnish is brushed on and a polish is applied with a rubber.

Spirit-based varnishes are made by using shellac, methylated spirits and possibly a kaurie gum or some other type of resin to improve one quality or another, good flow, quick drying, better adhesion, and so on. In my youth I often used white hard varnish for coating coffins after the first bodying process. This coat of varnish helped to hold up the second bodying process, ready for the final finish. The completed job was excellent, with very good film build and a brilliant gloss finish.

Two-can isocyanate polyurethane varnish
These varnishes are the modern polyurethane types and there are two in this group. One is a cold cure system and the other a catalyst curing isocyanate system. They are both mixed before application.

FIG 58 *Varnish kettle*

The cold cure system uses an isocyanate adduct such as trimethylol-propane which helps to make the isocyanate component of the system non-volatile. However the toxicity must be reduced by using a low volatile isocyanate called diphenylmethane di-isocyanate.

There is also a polyol component in this system which can either be polyester or polyether. The isocyanate reacts with water, atmosphere water vapour or any water which happens to be present on the substrates surface. This can cause softness within the film making it less resistant to chemicals. This problem can be reduced by adding extra isocyanate but unfortunately it creates a more brittle film but with increased chemical resistance.

The catalyst curing system includes an isocyanate-terminated prepolymer which is similar to the one-can moisture systems. The catalyst part of this system is usually an amine. With the introduction of some heat (stoving) the film forming is speeded up without adding extra catalyst. Longer pot life is possible with this system together with good flexibility and moisture resistance.

With these types of varnishes it is possible to have good chemical resistance, durability, high film strength and good adhesion. They are quite suitable for a very wide variety of substrates, especially oily timbers.

Varnish application

Varnishing needs skill and care for good results. When applying a varnish make sure you have all the necessary equipment – brushes, varnish, kettles, solvents and any other requisite tools. Firstly, pour the desired amount of varnish into a varnish kettle or an earthenware container. Dip the varnish mop into the kettle, taking care not to let the mop become immersed too deeply in the varnish. Apply the varnish by using diagonal strokes across each other, working quickly, then pulling out left to right. The final brushing should be done in the same direction to pull out the varnish cleanly. One word of warning: because varnish is free flowing, the varnish tends to find its own level after settling, so don't apply too much with your varnish mop or brush. Don't over-brush, just sufficient to pull out the varnish over the complete surface. Watch carefully any areas around carvings and mouldings which may have slight runs at the edges. Pull out the runs quickly before they dry. Remember, if coating new wood, the first coat will sink into the timber to some degree and will require a light sanding when dry. Build up the required coats when the first coat is dry. Normally two further coats will be adequate for a reasonable job.

Varnish application on new timber

There must be a sound base for varnish so the timber requires sizing if a good final flat varnished surface is to be produced. The size should be applied before varnishing, making sure that the work is quite clean in all corners, mouldings, carvings and highlights. Never apply too much size, just enough to dry out before any further process is undertaken. When dry, lightly sand down and then apply your first coat of varnish.

Varnishing on coloured work

One problem when varnishing is deciding what type of varnish to use on dyes or pigmented colours. Remember, there is a great variety of tinted varnishes. To retain your desired colour, whether it be a bright blue dye or a blue opaque colour you must choose the clearest varnish available. One of the best pale varnishes should be adequate for this purpose, especially the two-can isocyanate type or a pale one-can polyurethane.

Some of the older, more traditional oleoresinous varnishes are dark in colour and give brown or amber colours and if used over coloured dyes or pigments will tint and darken them. They should be avoided if full clarity of colour is required.

Varnishing on floors

Traditionally, cheap varnish stains were used on deal floor boards, which when damaged tended to chip easily and therefore show unsightly marks. It is possible to produce a really good, well-varnished floor with a good colour if better quality materials are used. The most important operation, of course, is proper sanding of the timber.

All too often this operation is ignored. Originally, deal floors were fitted and, of course, there are numerous knots and very rough areas which require sanding. If, however, we are to attempt such a floor which is made of maple (a ballroom floor), then life is much easier. Maple floors finish well and are quite the opposite to deal floors when it comes to preparation.

Floor preparation

Make sure that any rough areas are scraped, especially in corners which are difficult to reach with an electric sander. If you have used any solvents for washing off any floor adhesive, make sure the surface is clean and dry. Some adhesives tend to stain the timber, especially the bitumen type. Make sure the whole surface is clean, level, well-sanded and that all the dust is removed before attempting any staining or varnishing. The timber must be as clean as possible if you are to achieve a good finish.

Floor staining

Various shades of stains may be used – the choice is yours. It could be oak, walnut or mahogany or even a yellow pine. In my experience most floors are stained in a brown oak colour. Oil-ground colours are ideal to use, but, remember, they do show patchy streaks, especially on deal timbers. There are many proprietary stains on the market nowadays which give good colour and dry quite fast.

Some floors, teak for example, may not require staining because of its natural golden brown or mid-brown colour. A couple of coats of varnish is all that is required. However, if you do decide to stain a teak floor, a warm golden teak stain, usually on the weak side, should be adequate – just sufficient to brighten the timber.

Generally you can purchase almost any colour of stain. Five litres of stain should cover anything from 65–85 m^2 (213–279 square feet) depending on how porous the timber is. Always allow adequate drying and adopt the manufacturer's recommendations.

When applying your stains use a good quality stain brush, possibly a wide flat brush, and apply your stain in the direction of the grain, not across it, otherwise you could produce a bad patchy effect, especially on deal timbers. If, on the other hand, your floor is block flooring it will be hardwood, and if you apply your stain in one direction generally you should have no problem if you wipe off the surplus stain as you go along. Hardwood timbers generally like oil stains. Timbers sometimes used in the manufacture of block flooring are sapele, oak, maple, teak, utile and afrormosia.

When you are ready to apply your varnish, just follow the directions given for varnish application (p. 78).

Varnish mops and brushes

Varnish mops and brushes are the most important tools used when applying a good quality varnish. Make sure your mops and brushes are thoroughly clean before use, and because much finer and better quality bristles are used in the manufacture of varnish mops, it pays to look after them (see pp. 25).

Finishing on varnish (felting)

In very high class work where numerous coats of varnish have been applied, a 'felting down' is

carried out. A piece of felt or even a felt pad is rubbed over the varnished surface, together with an abrasive (such as pumice powder or fine carborundum powder mixed with water for lubrication).

Felting down can also be done with another tool instead of felt – namely, a fine soft shoe brush. Apply the pumice powder onto the shoe brush, smear a few drops of linseed oil over the varnished surface and work the brush over the surface, gently matting down the varnish, removing the gloss, until the surface is completely matt. Any excess oil can be removed with white spirit and finally cleaned off with a soft clean rag. Sometimes varnish surfaces are finished off dull instead of glossy.

Finishing on varnish (waxing)

Although varnish is normally left, either gloss from brush or mop application or even felted down wax can be applied to produce a satin effect. There are numerous waxes available, and only a good quality one should be used. Application can be by rag, simply polishing off the excess with a soft clean rag. However, if the floor is large, a floor-polisher can be used which will provide more weight to the floor area and also burnish the

FIG 59 *Dulling down a gloss finish with pumice powder and brush (polish or varnish)*

FIG 60 *The dulled finish after removing the pumice powder*

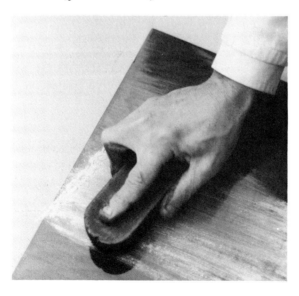

varnish to a good clean surface. Floor polishers of the industrial type are used in hospitals, factory canteens, dance halls, leisure centres, hotels and schools. The wax provides that extra protection to the varnish and therefore helps to give it longer life.

Finishing on old varnish

Sometimes it is necessary to restore an old varnished surface. Care must be taken to remove any old dirt, grease and grime which may have been left, especially in any mouldings, carvings, corners or crevices. Good quality soap solution in warm water should be used to remove these contaminants. Do not use boiling water or you may soften up the varnish. To apply your soap solution use an old mutton cloth and wash down really well. Make sure you use plenty of clean water to remove the soap solution and rinse down thoroughly.

Spirit varnishing

This varnish is less common today owing to the more popular use of faster drying dyes to which a polyurethane varnish can be applied. Spirit varnishes dry fast and can cause the amateur problems. It is best to use a spirit varnish on small items because of the fast drying solvent.

Spirit varnishes are much better to sand down than oil-bound varnishes. They are harder and therefore sand smoother. Any uneven surfaces on a spirit varnish can be smoothed by using white spirit or water as a lubricant. It pays to use a little knowledge of the French polisher when using spirit varnishes and to use the polishing rubber to level out any uneven patches on the varnished surface. Before applying a spirit varnish it is a good policy to apply one coat of French polish or size to help to seal the grain. This sealing coat can be lightly sanded before coating with spirit varnish.

Make sure you use good quality brushes for applying your spirit varnish. The camel hair variety should be used, and there are various sizes for various types of work. Use an earthenware container, or glass if this is unobtainable, for your varnish. Do not use any metal containers or brushes which have the hairs bound with metal.

The metal can have a bad effect on the varnish, turning it dark.

Exterior varnish finishing

Traditionally, French polish was used on many shopfronts, banks and some specialist exterior work. Because French polish is not weather proof, oil-based varnish was used to protect the polish. Normal polishing systems are adopted, filling in, bodying up, colouring and so on and then finally a good quality clear varnish is applied to protect the polish.

Exterior varnished shopfronts are a very rare sight nowadays and, of course, many shopfronts are finished with a polyurethane varnish and very badly at that. To obtain a really good exterior finish, adequate preparation is of paramount importance and this preparation is somewhat neglected. The open grain of the timber must be filled properly so that a smooth surface can be achieved by repeated coatings of polish and varnish.

The tendency today is to use a polyurethane varnish on open grain timber; because the grain is left unfilled, the varnish soon breaks down because there is no film thickness built up on a sound grain filled base. Consequently, the grain swells and the polyurethane cracks and flakes off very quickly.

Faults and defects in varnishing

Blooming

This whiteness appearing on varnished surfaces is known as 'bloom'. It is often seen on high quality good water resistant varnishes. The surface induces the moisture from the atmosphere. It usually appears when the varnish film is hard. However, because of varnish formulation, water can come from the gum which has been used during the varnish making and, of course, any varnish which has been stored in damp conditions could have a bloom on its surface when used.

Good ventilation is needed to prevent blooming; dry air is ideal. It is very difficult, of course, to have perfect conditions for varnishing and so a happy medium will suffice. To remove bloom, rub hard with olive oil and vinegar and remove any surplus, wiping the surface clean. If the bloom is due to poor quality varnish, then it is likely that you will have to strip off the varnish with a stripping solution. Obviously you will now have to re-varnish the whole work.

Cissing

Large holes appear in the varnish film caused by grease in the film. The fault does not belong to the varnish but to some contaminant that must have appeared before or during coating. If the problem is severe, you may have to strip off the varnish and re-finish.

Cracking

This is caused by using a varnish which is too brittle, has insufficient or excessive oil. In practice usually a hard varnish is applied over soft elastic varnish and because of expansion and contraction with temperature changes, each varnish pulls against the other, causing tensions within the film, resulting in cracking. If too much turpentine is used for thinning the varnish, then this could also cause cracking.

It may be possible to flat down the varnish and re-coat, if not severe.

Creeping

This happens when too much varnish is applied, and in cold conditions an uneven surface is produced which does not allow the varnish to level out. The only satisfactory remedy is to remove the varnish and re-coat. Sometimes, however, if the defect is not too severe it is sufficient to rub down with water and pumice powder, clean off and re-coat. This is highly unlikely though. Most varnished surfaces suffering from this defect need stripping.

Discoloration

This is probably caused by contamination of the varnish from iron coming into contact with the materials. Keep all varnishes away from metals.

Dull patches

Dull patches sometimes show up on a varnished surface, caused by poor sealing coats, poor quality timbers or absorption by some timbers of the varnish in certain areas. Uneven application of varnish can produce the same effect as well. The remedy is usually to apply another coat of varnish as evenly as possible.

Drying problems

Providing you prepare all your tools and varnishes correctly and work in reasonable conditions, you should have no drying problems. However, having said that, if any contaminant is around you may have problems. Make sure there is no oil in your mops and brushes, no grease on your work, and work in reasonably well ventilated areas if possible. Good warm air circulation is needed.

Flaking

Flaking occurs when varnish separates itself from previous coats, although this problem is not too common. It is probably caused by poor adhesion between coats and different types of varnish being used on one job. Other possible causes are poor pigments, moisture in the timber or even poor sealing coats. It is best to remove the varnish and re-finish.

Gritty surface

There are various causes for this. The varnish could have been stored badly, possibly in cold conditions or even attacked by frost. Of course the common cause is dirt whilst varnishing, possibly from dirty mops and brushes. Make sure they are well cleaned out before use.

Loss of gloss

Usually overthinning causes loss of gloss, that is, a varnish which has low solids for a given viscosity gives a very thin film with little body. Don't overthin a varnish.

Pock marks

These are by slight indentations in the varnish and are due to steam or warm moist air or even smoke in the atmosphere at the time the varnish is applied. Sometimes if too much turpentine is left in the varnish mop pock marks may appear. The remedy is to clean down the surface and re-varnish.

Ropey finish

Troubles can arise from the improper storage and use of varnishes. If the varnish is old or has been stored in cold conditions, then you are likely to come across this problem. Never use a hot varnish on a cold job, for example, on outside work such as a shopfront. The change in temperature will be no good for the varnish and could cause a ropey effect on application.

Streaks

Varnish streaks could be caused by poor mixing when formulation takes place. Driers, oils or turpentine in the varnish may cause this defect. To overcome the problem, try re-varnishing.

Wrinkling

An unbalanced drier incorporated in the varnish sometimes causes wrinkling if a thick coat is applied. It can also be caused if the varnish coat is not brushed out correctly. Always pull out the film sufficiently to avoid this defect.

Conclusion

In general, to avoid varnish defects it is obvious that cleanliness is most important. Because most varnishes are slow drying, you cannot get away with being too messy in your working area. Always try to keep the varnish alive at the edges when coating, don't let the varnish become too viscous. Apply evenly, level off carefully and level off to dry. Remember, your last coat should be straight, working in one direction only.

Good quality high class work should have at least three or four coats of varnish, and it is best to rub down the first coat to obtain a good flat base. Never mix different makes of varnish – stick to the same make. If you require a really good gloss use what is known as double coating. This method involves applying a top coat of varnish on top of the previous coat before it is dry. You must work quickly with the final coat so that you do not pull up the first coat. Obviously you will require a great deal of practice to produce good results here. It goes without saying that to obtain the best possible results you should use the best brushes available. There is no substitute.

CHAPTER NINE

Special finishing processes

●

Oak

In this chapter I propose to deal with special finishes other than the usual warm and cold colours which are usually applied on the more common timbers we know today. You will no doubt have found that oak timbers are very versatile because of their acidic nature. Oak will take a great variey of finishing materials and with careful selection, some skill and sometimes a little luck you may be able to produce some really delightful colours. Here are a few special finishes on oak timbers.

Decorative oak

Because oak has a deep grain structure many decorative colours can be applied in a pigmented grain filler. The main preparation of the timber is to open the grain with a steel wire brush so that the filler can be rubbed into the grain to its maximum depth. Stroke the wire brush along the natural length of the grain using a fair degree of pressure. Do not rub the wire brush across the grain otherwise you will scratch the timber beyond repair. When you are satisfied that the grain is opened up, sand down the timber with a medium grade garnet paper and dust off the surface when sanding is completed. If you are lucky enough to have air pressure available, you can blow out the excess dust with an air-line.

The next stage is to decide what base colour you require. Traditionally oak timbers are stained brown, either cold or warm. However, a bright colour such as green, blue, yellow can be effective. Bright colours are ideal for such items as wall panelling in restaurants, discos, offices and some shop fittings. The bright mixed solvent stains are ideal, although some of the water stains can be used too. But remember, water stains raise the grain and are slow drying.

Once you have decided on the colour, stain the whole job and allow the stain to dry thoroughly. Apply a thin coat of white polish to fix the stain and again allow adequate drying time. Lightly paper down the white polish, dust off the surface and, using a clean polishing rubber, apply a few rubbers of white polish. Do not fill in the grain with polish. When you have obtained a reasonable dull shine over the work, leave the surface to dry, preferably for at least four hours.

At this stage we are now ready to apply the pigmented filler. The colour of the filler will again depend on choice. The colours could range from white to black or any bright colour. A light background stain will probably have a dark filler applied and vice versa. Rub the selected filler into the grain making sure not to miss any of the open grain. Remove all the surplus filler with hessian and finally clean off with a clean rag. Allow adequate drying time for the filler before you make any attempt at finishing.

To finish off the work you may proceed in one of two ways. Either seal the filler with a thin coat of white polish and allow to dry for at least eight hours. The polish can be applied by polishing mop or rubber. If a rubber is used ensure that you apply the polish evenly, keeping the rubber moving in the direction of the grain. Alternatively, you can apply a white wax after the white polish so that a smooth satin finish is produced. Rub the wax well into the surface and polish off the surplus wax with a soft clean rag, rubbing hard. The work is now completed and you should have a bright oak colour with a decorative grain effect.

To produce the best results select the best grain in the oak timbers for any decorative grain effect. Oak is very expensive but if carefully selected the final results are really worthwhile.

Limed oak

This finish on oak is similar to the previous finish, except that the filler used also colours the timber, leaving a deposit in the pores of the grain. The preparation of the timber is exactly the same as for the decorative oak. Use a wire brush to open up the grain and remove all the dust.

FIG 61   *Opening the grain in oak timber with a wire brush*

FIG 62   *Applying liming paste on oak timber to fill the grain*

FIG 63   *Polishing off the surplus lime with a coarse rag*

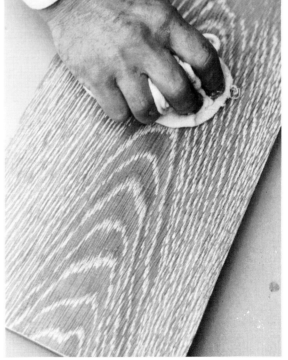

The next process is somewhat different as you use slaked lime. Mix about 1 kg (2 lb 3 oz) of unslaked lime (lump lime) in 1 litre (1½ pt) of water and allow the mixture to cool. After mixing, the mixture should resemble a normal patent filler. When the mixture is ready, rub it well into the pores of the grain working across the grain and allow the filler to become semi-dry. At this stage wipe off the surplus filler, working gently across the grain and then very lightly with the grain and allow the surface to dry out. When dry, rub down very lightly with a fine flour paper or fine garnet paper and apply one coat of white polish. When dry, lightly paper down, apply a few rubbers of white polish and after about eight hours rub white wax over the surface and polish off with a clean rag. If you wish to increase the whiteness in the grain, add some zinc white into the white wax. If this is unobtainable use a little titanium dioxide. Be careful, this white is very powerful.

The background colour produced by liming the oak will be a grey colour and can only be achieved by using these materials. A more modern method is to apply a uniform colour, say a grey stain, and then apply a white grain filler after sealing the stain. A matt or satin varnish can be used but remember the colour and finish will be entirely different from the traditional limed oak effect.

There are many variables concerning limed oak, some of which are mentioned in the previous section on decorative oak. There are numerous materials on the market, some of which are wax emulsions which incorporate an emulsifying alkali. When applied, this changes the colour of the timber through a chemical change.

The problem with coloured grain fillers, especially the white fillers, is that of deterioration due to contaminants – such as dirt, grime and staining. These finishes are very difficult to renovate and can prove to be very expensive if refinishing is required.

Weathered oak

This colour is an imitation of weathered oak and can be produced by using either builders' lime or a mixture of caustic soda and lime. Prepare the mixture and apply to the timber using a grass brush, working in the direction of the grain.

Allow adequate drying and lightly paper off the surplus with fine flour paper. Dust off and apply a matt wax, polishing off the surplus with a rag. Slight variations in colour can be achieved by using chloride of lime but the varying colours obtained are quite personal and depend on your own choice. Remember, oak is acidic, and any alkali will have its effect when applied. Some other materials which produce varying colours are soda water, sulphate of iron and copper sulphate.

It is worth remembering that a wax finish gives little protection so if a more resistant finish is desired, a matt varnish can be applied on the weathered oak. It all depends if the work is interior or exterior. Generally, weathered oak is used outside, so a simple waxing may be sufficient. Varnishes tend to peel off with exposure to the elements, especially on open grain timbers.

Fumed oak

In stables it was noted that oak timbers and pitch pine changed colour because of the ammonia in the atmosphere reacting with the acid in the wood. The imitation of this colour probably originated in Scotland, and was first used commercially by the Morton brothers. The process was known as fumed oak or art furniture.

To obtain a fumed oak colour you need a cabinet or possibly a room which can be sealed. The area required will depend upon the size of work to be fumed. A container, preferably glass or earthenware, is filled with ammonia (0.880 specific gravity) and placed in the cabinet or room in a central position. Ideally the room should have a glass door so that you can see the colour change taking place. The cabinet can have a hole cut into it and an oak peg placed in the hole for checking the colour. Remove the peg from time to time to examine the colour change.

To produce an even fumed colour, the furniture must have been made from selected oak, be free from any marks, especially grease marks and any drawers, cupboard doors, etc. must be left open. Do not cover up any timber which requires fuming otherwise the timber will not change colour.

If you are fuming work which is made out of different types of oak, then you should attempt to colour the light areas. This can be done by mixing some spirit black and bismark brown to make up a brown spirit colour. Mix this spirit brown in a little polish and colour out the light areas of the work. If there are any dark areas you will need to bleach these using oxalic acid or the two-can bleaches, depending on how dark the area is. Remember to neutralize the bleaching agents with water to clean out any surplus chemicals.

When the desired colour is achieved apply a protective coating. Usually a coat of white polish is applied, lightly papered down with flour paper, and then one or two thin rubbers of white polish will complete the work, giving a dull shine. If a smooth satin texture is required, rub over the work with wax polish, polishing off the surplus wax with a soft clean cloth.

Sometimes the work can be partially bodied up with white polish, left to dry for about eight to twelve hours, then dulled down with pumice powder applied with a stiff brush. Polish off the surplus pumice powder with a soft rag.

Some points worth noting are that because of the nature of the timber, it is difficult to control the colour and no exact time can be given for completion of the fuming process. Anything from 12–24 hours may be required. Obviously, this process is a dry one since no liquid actually touches the timber. The finish colour is again up to you and is really quite easy to produce. Apart from the normal white polish and wax finishes you can apply raw linseed oil on the fumed oak. This oil produces a nice rich colour and when the surplus oil is wiped off and the surface is allowed to dry a thin coat of polish can be applied.

Finally, as previously mentioned, selected oak is the ideal choice and one that is good for fuming is Japanese oak. If any of the American or Canadian oaks are used you will see that ammonia has little effect. These oaks will require some form of colouring and a commercial fumed oak stain can be used. Of course, this is not the traditional fuming method but a substitute colour. There is little call for this special colour today, but when the timber is specially selected and the work is fumed and finished correctly the results are really worthwhile.

Bog oak

This gives the appearance of a dull black colour and may be achieved by mixing various colours together. Usually a combination of green, black and red stains will do the trick. A typical finishing system would be to apply the mixed stain, allow to dry, apply one coat of polish, match up to the desired colour and then apply a dark grain filler. Allow the filler to dry and finish off with a coat of polish, then wax down with matt wax, polishing off with a soft rag. There are variations on the above system using a range of stains and grain fillers, but the choice of materials will often depend on the colour required and the nature of the timber.

Pollard oak

Because some oak timbers, especially English brown oak, vary in colour it may be necessary to darken down the light areas with a bichromate of potash stain, which should be mixed fairly weak. When applying your grain filler, add a little brown umber just to darken down the normal golden oak filler. The normal finishing system for golden oak should be adopted but do not use any red polish in the final finishing stage. Spirit out the work after the bodying process using a good transparent polish.

Pollard oak is an unusual colour and very rarely seen today, except in some furniture auction rooms. However, it is a good, effective colour. Again, the colour is a matter of choice but well-selected oak timbers are required.

Flemish oak

This is sometimes seen in churches and is usually a dark brown, coffee colour. To produce this special colour we use bichromate of potash. Mix about $\frac{1}{2}$ kg (1 lb 2 oz) in 10 l (15 pt) of water and when mixed allow to stand for about an hour. Strain the mixture to obtain a good clear stain. Apply the stain to the timber using a stiff brush and make sure you work with the grain to produce an even colour. Remember, bichromate of potash being a chemical stain, strikes immediately and if applied across the grain will show unsightly patches. Allow the stain to dry; the grain will have risen so you will need to lightly sand down the surface with fine flour paper before any finish is applied.

Now to produce the dark coffee colour use a number of stains – a dark brown oil stain, a black stain or even the much faster drying mixed solvent stains. Whatever stain you decide to apply, allow adequate drying after wiping off the surplus. When dry, apply one or two coats of orange polish allowing this to dry before papering down with fine garnet paper. When adequate papering is completed, the surface should not be cut back with pumice powder and linseed oil which will smooth out the surface and produce a dark rich colour. Make sure you remove all the surplus oil by rubbing with a clean rag. When complete, no further work is needed and if any maintenance is done, just rub over with a rag.

If you look at the oak timbers in some churches, you will notice that the timber is specially cut for this particular finish. Usually quarter sawn brown oak is used, yet again another special finish very rarely seen today.

Bleached oak

Many shopfittings were finished in a bleached colour, especially showcases. Unfortunately the colour tends to fade after a time but can still look quite attractive if looked after. Use quartered oak and straight grained oak for this, matching it well for best results.

Use the fast acting A and B bleaches for best results. Apply the A solution first and when partially dry apply the B solution. The surface will begin to react showing a slight effervescing; when this has settled, wash off the surplus bleach with plenty of cold water. Make sure you wash out the grain properly to remove any excess bleaching agents in the grain and allow the timber to dry out before any further finishing is undertaken. When dry, use white polish to seal the timber. Lightly paper down with fine flour paper and proceed to fill in the grain with a light oak grain filler. You can use a little yellow ochre in the filler if you require a slightly paler yellow oak but remember, the colour will tone down with age. When the filler has dried out, apply a further coat of white polish, paper down again, body up and finish off with the stiffing out process. If you require a

much brighter glossy finish, the final stiffing out can be done with transparent polish.

Grey oak

A light grey oak colour can be produced by using a ready prepared stain which is slightly pigmented. The stain can either be oil-based or water-based. The secret in applying these stains is to wash coat the timber, allow it to partially dry and then wipe off the surplus stain very lightly, keeping your wiping rag working with the grain. The ideal finish should be matt or satin. These finishes can be obtained by applying white polish onto the stain and the final finish should be stiffed out with a white polish rubber. Similar to finishing bog oak, you can apply a matt wax to give it that smooth texture.

Oak colour variations

Having a complete range of stains and grain fillers provides the woodfinisher with the opportunity to produce a vast range of oak colours, and with knowledge of these materials it is possible to produce almost any colour. Don't forget to experiment first with scrap off-cuts of oak.

Chemical stains such as bichromate of potash, sulphate of iron and the oak oil stains should be the old standbys. Some antique effects can be produced by using ammonia and an oil stain washed in afterwards. Some aniline dyes can also be used but remember, they are difficult to use on large areas. Don't forget: always apply a water stain first and any oil, spirit or mixed solvent stain second. Remember to paper down lightly any water stain which will have raised the grain. Of course, if you have proceeded correctly, you will have damped down the timber first before applying any water stains. It all depends on how you have tackled the job in hand.

Ebonizing

This is probably known as black polishing in the woodfinishing trade as well as ebonizing. Personally I dislike black staining or polished work because it heavily stains the hands and takes a long time to clean off. Ebonizing is not an easy finish to produce because of the various black colours achieved by using different black stains, dyes and polishes. A great deal of skill is required when using black colours because it is very easy to work through the colour, especially on edges, carvings and mouldings. If you do work through the colour, then re-staining and polishing is needed and the work is held up while the repair dries out.

Some of the materials used to produce an ebony colour are somewhat complex and the process to achieve the final finish can be very lengthy indeed. Generally, close grain whitewood timbers were used when any ebonizing was done: timbers such as apple, pear, cherry, sycamore, holly, whitewood and any of the closer grained mahoganies are suitable.

To prepare the timber make sure that there are no grease marks on the surface by wiping it over with vinegar and water or a very weak solution of ammonia. Failing that, a weak bleaching agent will be adequate; household bleach will do. Of course the grain will have risen slightly so paper down the surface before the next process.

You then need a strong black stain. One of the best is vegetable black, a good dense black for ebonizing. Mix between 100–200 g (3.5–7 oz) of vegetable black to $\frac{1}{2}$ l (15 fl oz) of water. When well mixed apply this stain over the whole work and allow to dry. If you require the stain to be more stable, you may mix in a little glue size. This will also help to seal the timber.

When this stain is completely dry prepare the aniline dyes. Mix 50 g (2 oz) of aniline black in 0.25 l (8 fl oz) of methylated spirits to which you should also add about 0.15 l (5 fl oz) of polish. Mix all the materials together and then strain them carefully through a fine cheesecloth and bottle up ready for use. Some polishers tended to like a blue-black shade, for which you need to add a little spirit blue to the strained mixture. Mix up again and apply one coat with a polish mop to the whole surface, working in straight lines from left to right. You will now have two coats of black on your work – one black water stain and one black spirit stain. When the second coat has dried out, lightly paper the work down with fine flour paper and apply a black matt wax all over the work. Polish off the surplus and allow to dry. This will

give a smooth texture to the final finish. If a much drier texture is required, leave the second coat to dry after coating with the polish mop and lightly rub down the surface with the back side of an old piece of abrasive paper.

You will find that there are numerous blacks to be obtained. One other black is gas black which gives a good clear colour and hides the grain quite well. Another black is drop black sometimes known as Berlin black, which dries dull and is also used for lettering. Whatever black you decide to use, stick to the same one throughout the work to avoid colour variations in the completed work.

For the final process you may need to produce a high gloss finish; this is obtained with the normal bodying up using black polish. Complete the work with transparent polish, using the stiffing out and spiriting out methods. If you need to fill in any partially open grain timbers such as the mahoganies, then use a black filler. A black filler can be made by adding a little vegetable black to any dark brown filler and mixing well before application.

Probably the quickest way to produce an ebony colour is to use the black aniline dye. Apply the black stain to the timber and allow to dry. Using a polishing mop, coat the complete job with a coat of black polish. Take care not to lift off the aniline black. It is possible you may do so in one or two areas but if you do, don't worry, you can re-coat these areas later. For the bodying up process add some gas black to your polish to give you a good solid black. The final finishing should be done with the normal spirit black becase gas black is really a dark brown black whereas the spirit black is a blue-black colour.

Any matting down of a gloss black finish can be done by using pumice powder with a little Berlin black added. Remember, black matt finishes show finger marks but they can be matted down again at any time.

Enamelling

Today the woodfinisher comes across more pigmented finishes than ever before. In modern finishing we use the term 'pigmented lacquers' or 'enamels'. Briefly, they are simply coloured finishes which obliterate the grain of the timber in either matt, satin or gloss finishes.

When dealing with old furniture the enamels used were spirit-based, and after the timber was coated with a spirit enamel colour you could apply a polish to finish off the work, usually a transparent finishing polish. The benefit of using spirit enamels was that they were fast-drying compared with oil-based enamels. Normally cheaper types of timber were used for spirit enamelling, and the enamel was applied by brush, polish mop, or fine camel hair colour brush.

Spirit enamels could be purchased already made, and some of the more common colours were pale blue, green, lemon yellow and white. The enamels needed to be well-mixed before use, and application was by layer upon layer, allowing fine papering down between coats. Fine silicone carbide paper is ideal, grades 400 or 600 giving a fine cut to the surface.

Make sure you build up the film thickness to a good density to allow for adequate papering down. The final finishing can be transparent polish or a transparent spirit varnish. The polish or varnish can be lightly tinted with the desired colour, blue, green, lemon or white. You should lightly paper again between coats, except the final coat if finished by brush. You can, however, finish off with one or two rubbers of transparent polish just to give the work that extra smooth texture.

You must take care not to lift the colour if you use the finishing method.

One point worth mentioning is the possibility of needing a sealing coat on open grain timbers. A good, white shellac sealer will do the trick, and a light sanding will provide you with a good base for the enamelling process. One or two coats may be required but this will depend on the nature of the timber.

Before any large scale work is done practise on sample pieces of timber and then small items to get the feel of using spirit enamels. Remember, spirit enamels dry fast and careful application is required. Try to apply the enamels quickly and evenly, working straight from left to right. Thin coats should be applied, not thick ones.

Although spirit enamelling is no longer practised, there is no reason why you should not attempt to produce some finishes using these materials. They can have their place on small items, such as clock cases, toys, jewellery boxes and so on.

Scumbling

For this particular finish you need a background colour of your choosing, and to achieve good results it is better if you have some artistic skills in the use of colour application.

Scumbling consists of applying a stain on a base

FIG 64   *Two examples of Italian scumble*

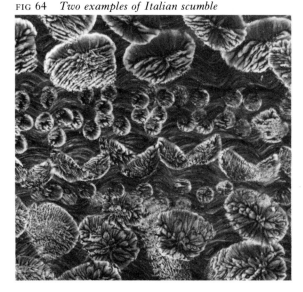
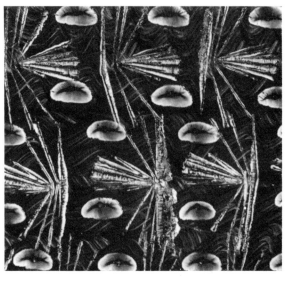

colour. The base colour will be opaque, and the stain will be applied wet onto the dry base colour. The wet stain will be wiped off in certain areas to expose the base colour. The stains used for this method are oil and water stains and they are applied by rag for the oil stain (any excess being removed with a cotton cloth), and a damp chamois leather for the water stain. You will need to change the position of the cloth or leather from time to time so that you are using the clean parts. Try to keep the cloths or leather taut whilst in use, keeping your thumb in the centre, twisting your thumb from left to right in small circles, giving you a swirl effect. You can choose various stain colours and by applying a range of colours on top of each other you will produce many pleasing effects. The colours will merge into each other producing a finishing texture which is known as 'scumbling'.

Much scumbling work is done on carvings, especially on pine timbers with a base colour or relief work. Scumbling can also be done with oil-based 'ready mixed' scumbles of various colours. These oil-based scumbles are more viscous than oil or water stains and if you choose to use them you will find that they take much longer to dry and are a little more difficult to wipe off because of the oil. Allow adequate drying before any final finishing is done.

When the scumble is completely dry apply a coat of polish or varnish by a polish mop or varnish mop. Generally, gloss finishes are used on scumble work, but there is no reason why a matt or satin finish should not be applied. The finish will depend on taste and décor. At the time of writing scumble work seems to be quite popular and even bright colours such as pale blues and pinks are being used for the background colour on such items as chairs, small cabinets, bedside lamps, small chests of drawers and picture and mirror frames.

Set in the right décor, scumble work can look very attractive. If you decide to attempt a variety of colours and artistic patterns, it is wise to practise a great deal before venturing on any good quality furniture. Choose your colours carefully and don't be afraid to experiment. You should find that the pale tones generally look more accep-

table. However, darker tones also look good in certain settings.

Graining

The woodfinisher will sometimes need to simulate a particular grain pattern. He will require all his skills related to the knowledge of colours, polishes, timbers and use of tools. Quite often the woodfinisher needs to imitate a grain pattern on sapwood or some different timber which had been used on a particular furniture piece. Unlike graining exercised by the decorator, the woodfinisher uses much faster drying materials and needs to work much quicker to complete his simulated grain effect. He needs to apply his colours quickly using his brushes with the skills of an artist. He needs to use his hands very quickly. Although brushes are usually used, such items as rags, feathers and soft sponges are also used.

Similar to scumbling, the skill of stroking the brush or other implement determines the outcome of the grain effect. Again, you will need to practise. Always determine the grain simulation while the stain is wet. Probably one of the best timbers to attempt to simulate is rosewood. Because the nature of the grain is strong, the colours are dark and the grain structure is heavy, you should find this timber much better to prac-

FIG 65 *Simulating pine grain with a fine pencil brush and spirit colour*

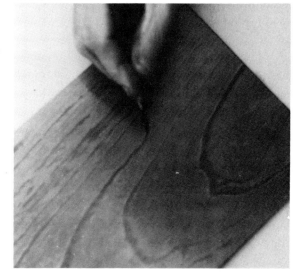

tise copying. You should use a medium brown mahogany base colour with an over grain of vandyke brown stain. Allow each application of stain to dry a little before over coating. Remember, stains can bleed into each other, so take care.

Generally there are two methods of graining – oil graining and water graining. Obviously owing to the length of time oil-based materials take to dry, this method will be slow. Water graining is quicker but, of course, the grain will rise with the water. Always damp down the timber before using this method; it will help a little.

If you can obtain decorators' graining tools you will find simulating various grains easier. The decorator uses a whole range of graining tools, including an overgrainer, a mottler, cutter, steel comb, rubber comb, pencil overgrainer, flat pitch, pencil brush, veining horn check roller, fan fitch and an improvised overgrainer usually made from an old paint brush. Also try to join a class of students learning the art of graining so that a skilled instructor can show you how to master the

tools mentioned. Although the woodfinisher does not normally use the decorators' graining tools, they can be of use under certain circumstances, for example, simulating the grain effects of oak, a difficult timber to imitate. The more aids you have the better the outcome.

Finishing is similar to scumbling. Use a clear transparent varnish or polish and build up the surface. Again, gloss finishes are acceptable but the choice is yours. If any tinting is required you can use the coloured polishes, orange, button, garnet and so on.

Marble finishes

These finishes are an attempt to reproduce the original marble veined colours on timber and require artistic skills. Firstly you need a base colour, which is usually a flat paint that has been sanded down well. The sanding can be done by using silicone carbide paper, usually grade 400, and a little soap and water or white spirit, which

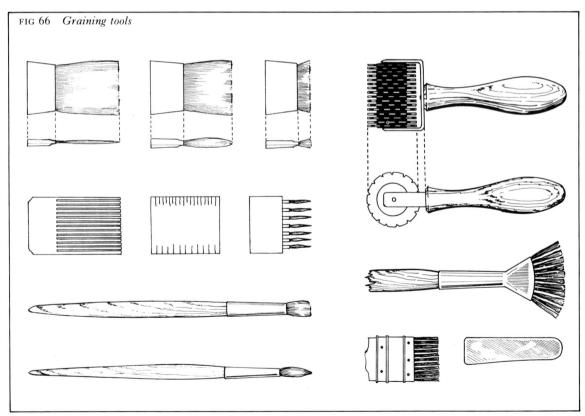

FIG 66 *Graining tools*

will help to produce a very flat, smooth surface. Make sure you dry off the surface before proceeding with the next stage.

Then apply a protective coating of shellac with a good quality polish mop and lightly sand it down when dry. Apply one or two light rubbers of shellac just to give you that final smooth texture to the surface. The surface must be very smooth before any attempt at marbling is done.

You will require some special tools and materials to produce your marble effects. These are: an old stiff paint brush; old turkey or phea-sant feathers; mutton cloth, about 40–50 cm (16–20 sq in); small sponges; some old news-papers; fine pencil brushes; and two oxhair brushes, one 6 mm ($\frac{1}{4}$ in) and one 13 mm ($\frac{1}{2}$ in).

Producing a marble effect

When you have prepared your base colour you are ready to produce the marble effect. This can be done in various ways. One method is to use the oxhair brushes, dip them into a slow drying, oil-based paint (with a little drying oil added) and hold the two brushes together as one. Apply the

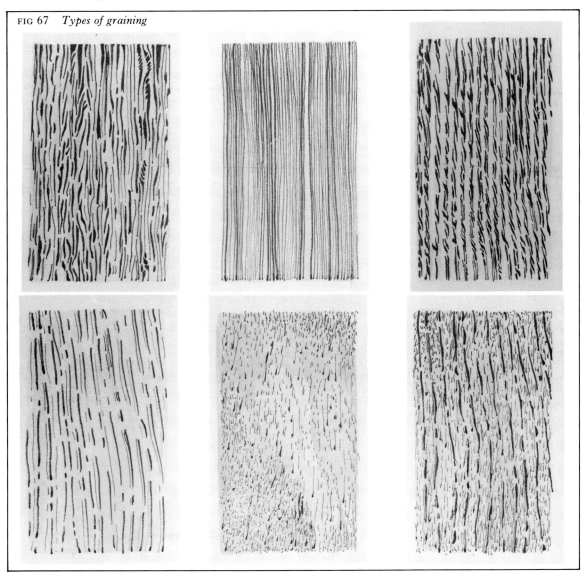

FIG 67   *Types of graining*

93

paint onto the base colour by tapping the paint lightly onto the surface, thus allowing the two colours (one from each brush) to merge together.

A second method is to use a mutton cloth which should be twisted around tightly, dipped into the marble colours required (which could be two or three different colours) and simply rolled over the base colour again and again, re-charging the mutton cloth as required.

A third method is to use old feathers which have been lightly clipped at the edges. Apply the shaded colour by laying the feathers very lightly over the surface to paint on the shade effect. You can use different feathers with different colours.

A fourth method is to use a stiff brush which has been lightly dipped in one or two areas of the bristles. Each dipped area may be charged with a different colour and then applied to the surface by a twisting and turning motion over the whole surface area.

Finally, you may also use sponges or newspapers which can be charged with the required colour and simply rolled or dabbed over the surface.

You will require a great deal of practice to overcome the application problems, so it is advisable to use a marble pattern to copy from. Scrap timber samples or even plain white cardboard which has been sealed will help you to produce a range of coloured samples. It is possible that you

FIG 68   *An example of a marble simulation*

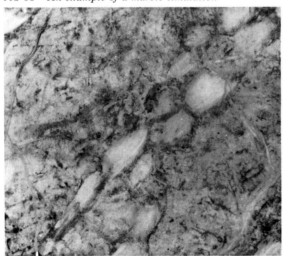

will be dismayed by some of your efforts, but persevere and you will succeed eventually.

One or two points worth noting are don't charge your brushes or feathers with too much colour, thus flooding the surface with too much colour. Turpentine or a little terebine will help to produce those special marble effects. Just apply a few drops of either in certain areas allowing the pools to be created and then just simply let the colours dry out. You may notice one or two areas later which require further attention; using the same tools and materials you can touch up these areas until you are satisfied with the outcome.

To complete the marble effect apply a light veining here and there. To do this, use a fine pencil brush which has been dipped into a thin oil-based paint, usually a dark colour, and paint the vein effect over the desired areas while the base marble colours are still wet, varying your stroke of the brush. Allow the work to dry out completely – this may be up to a week. Finally coat the work with best quality oil-based varnish. Usually gloss varnish is used but again the texture of finish will depend on your own personal choice.

Pine

Pickled pine

Although pine timbers are not all that popular today compared with the early twentieth century, it is worth mentioning some methods of finishing such timbers. To produce a 'pickled pine' finish, the whole work should be coated with nitric acid and water, mixed to a ratio of one part acid to eight parts water. The mixture really depends on the required colour. The colour of the pine will either be light or dark grey. It is always best to try out the mixture on a few scrap pieces of pine.

When making up the acid and water mixture, remember to add the acid to the water for safety purposes. Use rubber gloves to protect your hands and wear an apron. When using acid mixtures work carefully to avoid any damage which may occur from splashes.

To apply the acid use an old paint brush and apply a thin coating over the pine and allow the acid to dry out. You should see a change in colour; the tone of the pine should now be grey, and if you decide to shade any areas of the pine, you should lightly sand down the areas required and lighter areas will appear. The old paint brush should be well washed out with cold water as soon as possible after use.

Normally, when the acid finish has been applied a certain amount of 'distressing' (simulating marks of age and wear) is done, and then the work is lightly wiped over with a weak mixture of bichromate of potash and water mixed to a ratio of one part bichromate to six parts water. The bichromate mixture imparts a slight yellow tint to the pine. It is advisable to test the mixture on some scrap pine which has been treated similarly before applying the mixture on the work. When the mixture is dry, lightly paper down with flour paper and apply one coat of white polish. If you have pickled the pine correctly it will be a grey colour with a kind of yellowy cream colour in certain areas, which should look really attractive. When the white polish is dry, lightly paper down again and body up with white polish, stiffing out when a good body has been applied. Allow the work to dry out thoroughly overnight and cut down the polish with grade 000 steel wool. Then complete the work with a good polishing by using a wax rubbed over with a coarse rag. One of the good quality blended waxes will do the job. Make sure you polish off all the surplus wax.

Waxed pine

Most pine furniture today is sprayed with a matt or satin clear lacquer, whereas traditionally the pine was coloured with a strong bichromate of potash mixture, possibly about twice the normal strength of that for pickling pine. When the mixture is dry, the work is lightly sanded and then completed in exactly the same way as for pickled pine. The colour produced should be a very deep cream with a really rich satin finish.

Finishing other types of pine

There are other pine timbers you may come across including yellow pine, oregon pine and of course the common red deal. It is best to finish these timbers in their natural colour. A thin coat of white shellac sealer can be applied, lightly papered down with fine garnet paper when dry. Then wipe off the dust and apply one or two coats of gloss or satin oil-based varnish. The polyurethane type can be used if required. Some pine and the red deal timbers are often used on floors and these timbers are ideal for finishing with this method. If you require a darker pine, you can apply a modern coloured stain before sealing with the white shellac sealer and then finish off with the varnish as before.

Finishing plywood

Because plywood is produced from different veneers and the texture of the face veneer can sometimes be unpredictable it can be difficult to colour. Some of the birch plywood veneers absorb certain stains, particularly oil stains, so it is better not to use them. A coloured water stain is preferable to these plywood veneers. Also some of the mixed solvent stains are useful for applying on some plywood veneers.

The difficulty in staining plywoods is to produce uniformity of colour. Always work as quickly as possible, working systematically from left to right wiping off the excess stain as you go. Remember to overlap each coat of stain keeping the edges wet if possible.

When staining is completed you must seal the plywood. Again, this may be troublesome owing to the nature of the veneer surfaces. The surface area of plywood veneers tends to be rough, uneven and sometimes spongy. When any surface coatings are applied, certain areas of the plywood absorb the coating just like a sponge, causing dry fuzzy areas. One method of attempting to combat this problem is to apply a thin filler wash coat before sealing. The wash coat should be either natural or of a similar colour to the stain used. Make sure you remove all the surplus wash filler and allow it to dry out before any further coatings are applied.

To complete the work, any surface coating can be applied, including the oil-based varnishes, spirit varnishes and, of course, the range of polishes. The most important point though is the thorough cleaning up of the face veneer. Adequate scraping and sanding should be done before any staining or filling. You will also need to deal with any knots, knife cuts from rotary cutting of the veneers and any splits in the veneer surface.

CHAPTER TEN

Antique furniture finishing

●

Colour

Finishes on genuine antique furniture requires very little restoration unless a great deal of work has been done on the carcass or panelling. The colour of the finished work is very important, and great care must be taken to retain the beauty of the wood.

Faded colour

Generally you will find that most of the colour is in the timber itself if the furniture is in good condition and any repair work undertaken should preserve the patina in the timber if possible. This is not an easy job: the depth of colour is very fine and any sanding will remove that colour leaving a lighter appearance on the timber surface. However, you can replace the colour to some extent by using various chemicals and bleaches.

Use bleach if a restorer has replaced a piece of timber in a faded section of a furniture piece, thus leaving a much darker area that needs lightening. The next stage would be to use a dye or stain or a combination of both, usually on the bleached part in order to produce a good colour match before finishing. Remember to neutralize any bleaching agents if you choose to use this method.

When choosing colours for restoring a faded colour, choose with care. Water stains are good for new timbers, especially the vandyke crystals or powder, and the mahogany water stain as well. The stronger oil and spirit stains have good colour but sometimes fade, especially the spirit red col-

ours. These colours often turn to a cold yellowy effect after a few weeks, especially if the work is left in strong sunlight.

Try not to use pigment colours if at all possible. They obliterate and also change colour. If you must use them, use them sparingly. Also, always build up your colours carefully onto each other.

Restoring a faded colour

The most important first step when attempting to restore an existing surface is to find out what is actually on the surface. Use warm water and soap or a weak solvent solution such as linseed oil and turps substitute, mixed at a ratio of one part linseed oil to three parts turps substitute. You should find that with a little rubbing you will remove all the dirt and grime; for difficult areas, use a fine pumice powder or a felt pad or rag.

When removing the dirt and grime, take care not to rub through the old polished surface otherwise you will produce light patches within the polished surface which would then need restoring. Remember, you must attempt to retain the original patina and after the work is finally polished you will see that the natural colour and beauty of the timber will show through.

You may find that a more drastic method needs to be adopted in removing the dirt. If so, use methylated spirits with a fine steel wool, grade 000 and rub over the surface with the methylated spirits until the dirt is removed. Take care not to rub too hard, otherwise you will remove the old polish. When the dirt is completely removed, allow the surface to dry out thoroughly, lightly paper down with fine flour paper, clean off the dust from the abrasive action and then apply one coat of special pale polish or transparent polish. By doing this we are simply sealing the work ready for finishing. The finishing process can simply be a few light rubbers of special polish which must be allowed to dry. Do not attempt to body up the surface whatsoever – you simply need a thin film of polish just to seal the natural patina of the timber.

When the polish has dried out – this usually takes 12 hours – apply a wax dressing over the polish with a soft rag, rubbing off the surplus. Make sure you rub the wax well into the polish using plenty of pressure. Take care when applying the wax so that you produce a brilliant smooth glossy surface.

Reproduced antique finish

Today reproduction furniture is very popular, and you will see a good range of 'distressed' reproduction furniture in all the major furniture showrooms. In this chapter I shall attempt to deal with the three traditional timbers used in reproduction furniture, oak, mahogany and walnut.

Reproduction oak
Assuming the oak piece is completely new, we must consider the age of the piece or period or possibly consider what the customer might want.

The first step is to distress the work according to the relevant age required. The work could be solid oak panelled in the Tudor period or even a more up-to-date late Victorian period.

To produce the 'aged' look, a whole range of tools will be used, some of which are spokeshaves, rasps and files to produce wear on the corners, stretcher rails and feet. Abrasive papers are used to round off edges on drawers, doors and mouldings, then the rasp or spokeshave marks can also be removed with the abrasive papers. On the stretcher rails and feet or legs a chain is used to produce bruises which would have appeared by constant kicking. Edges of feet are roughened by an old stone or beaten with a hammer. When all the necessary wear and tear is completed a quick rub over with medium grade garnet paper will help to roughen up the timber ready for the next process called pickling.

The whole work is now pickled in a mixture of caustic soda and lime water. The ratio of mix is roughly 120 g (4 oz) of caustic soda to 1.5 l (2 pt) of lime water, which, when allowed to stand for about half an hour, should be strained off through a muslin and then a further 1.5 l (2 pt) of cold water should be added.

When applying the pickling solution cover the whole area as quickly as possible, working evenly with the grain, trying not to leave any patches at or near the edges. Keep the work wet all over. A darker colour can be produced by adding a little ammonia to the pickling solution or, if you prefer a lighter colour then use chloride of lime about

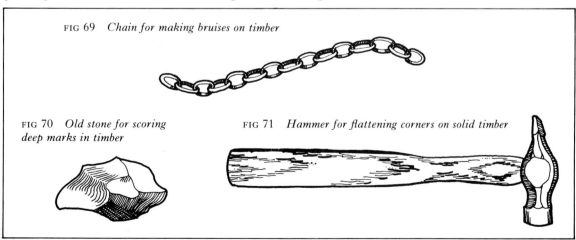

FIG 69   *Chain for making bruises on timber*

FIG 70   *Old stone for scoring deep marks in timber*

FIG 71   *Hammer for flattening corners on solid timber*

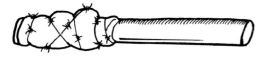

FIG 72   *Barbed wire stick for making scratch marks*

FIG 73   *Brush for applying antique wax*

FIG 74   *Blowlamp to dry out 'pickling process'*

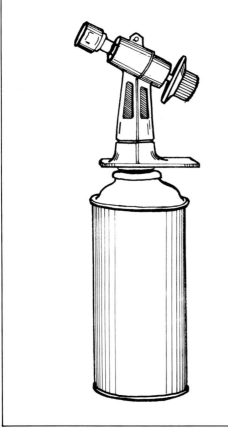

30–40 g (1 oz). You will find that most of the European oaks respond to this pickling process. Any American oak will require an addition of tannic acid to produce the desired colour. Test the acid before using it on the oak.

When the timber is pickled you must clean down the whole job. Wash it down completely with clean water and wipe off any surplus water. Allow to dry thoroughly so that you have an oak piece of furniture with a dark reddish colour. It must be emphasized that thorough cleaning down is an absolute must, otherwise unsightly white patches will show through in a few weeks' time. When dry, lightly paper down with fine garnet paper and lightly pass over the surface of the timber with a blow lamp to remove any rough areas of timber or splinters which may still be there from distressing.

The finishing can now commence. Stain the work with a water stain of the desired colour, wetting in the panel work, leaving the edges dark. You can use the same caustic soda for staining, if so desired, and add a few vandyke crystals or powder just to give a darker brown colour. A further drying off with the blow lamp will help to produce the desired colour effect and then lightly paper down with fine flour paper. All the interior work, if any, will simply need a thin coat of polish, thinned with methylated spirits, allowed to dry out overnight, lightly papered down, then thinly waxed and finally dusted with rottenstone and wiped off clean.

The next stage is to complete the work by polishing. Apply a thin coat of white polish or pale polish if you require the grey colour and a garnet polish if a browner colour is required. The colour should now be quite bright with a dull shine showing on the surface. At this stage any further distressing may be done. For instance, you may require a few bruises, scratches, water or heat marks to be made. To produce a few scratches, use a short piece of a broom handle. Wrap the end with a piece of tightly-bound rag, cover the rag with a small piece of barbed wire, fixing firmly, then draw or hit the surface of the timber with this tool. Alternatively, lightly roll it over the surface to make scratches, light marks and small dents. Take care not to produce any particular pattern by working systematically. You should attempt to distress the work only where the work would be naturally worn.

To produce heat marks, stand a cup of hot water on the surface until heat marks appear. Hot water can be left on the surface to produce the water marks. Sometimes even ink marks are produced by splashing black, blue or red ink, especially on the interiors of writing bureaux or desks.

To complete the final distressing, a quick wash coat of weak filler stain can be applied all over the work just to stain in the marks which have been applied. The aim is to make all the bruises, marks and scratches look much older than if left from the distressing tools. When all the filler stain is wiped off, allow adequate drying and then apply one coat of polish. When the polish has dried out, lightly paper down with fine flour paper and apply a few rubbers of polish, working straight with the grain. Now allow the work to stand for at least eight hours.

The work is now completed by applying a good quality wax, rubbing it well into the surface and using a soft shoe brush to brush out any mouldings or carvings. Finally, use grade 0000 steel wool to finish off the work and then rub over the whole work again with a hard wax containing carnauba wax and beeswax to give that much harder finished surface. Polish off all the surplus wax and if you require a much flatter finish you can use rottenstone to produce a much older look. The work is now complete.

In conclusion, I must stress that to produce distressed furniture requires a certain amount of skill and, of course, cabinet makers and skilled furniture makers can produce the necessary wear for the polisher to finish. Normally the polisher would not distress the furniture but only apply the aged look by using his skills and materials.

Reproduction mahogany and walnut

These two timbers can be treated similarly and assuming you receive the work from the cabinet maker ready distressed you should have little difficulty in producing the aged look by pickling. Any oak parts, drawers, etc. are pickled in exactly the same way as reproduction oak. Make sure you

wash off all the pickling solution as previously described.

With mahogany and walnut timbers, however, use less pickling solution and dry off the timber surface more quickly. This is because you are working with finer veneers and timbers that move and bind if too much water is applied. The water can be dried off with the blowlamp. Any pine timbers used may also be treated as for pickled pine and must also be dried out quickly.

To finish the interiors of these timbers use rottenstone darkened with a little gas black. Also, coat drawer runners with a thin coat of polish, allow to dry, paper lightly and wax over with a soft wax, polishing off the surplus. All drawer interiors can be coated with a mixture of Venetian red and white polish. Use just sufficient Venetian red to tint the polish. Allow the tinted polish to dry hard, paper down lightly and apply a rubber of white polish to smooth down the surface. When dry, apply a brown wax rubbing well into the surface and polish off the surplus. Finish off again with a further rubbing the following day to remove any wax that may not have been polished off sufficiently.

To produce the faded colour on the cabinet exteriors, it is best to use a bleaching agent; oxalic acid and water is weak enough to produce this faded colour. Mix the solution by diluting a saturated solution of oxalic acid and cold water with two thirds its own volume of water. Do not use a stronger solution otherwise you may have trouble with lifting veneers if water-based glues have been used. The saturated solution is mixed simply by dissolving the oxalic acid crystals in cold water until the water will dissolve no more crystals. Apply the solution to the timber. The method used is as for bleaching. Dry out the surface quickly with the blowlamp and apply a coat of white polish. When dry you should find that the surface is a little too dark, so further shading will be necessary until the correct colour is achieved. Generally it is advisable to finish with a colour slightly on the lighter side.

Do not fill the grain with a woodfiller, but if you decide to enhance the colour use a weak wash filler so that you do not leave too much colour in the grain. After bleaching remember the neutralizing process and use clean water.

Any distressing can now be done with the usual tools, but in this case do not distress too heavily. In general, mahogany and walnut timbers are not as heavily distressed as oak timbers so use your tools carefully. Coat the work with white polish, apply the required marks and scratches with the barbed wire stick, lightly paper down with fine flour paper and then polish over with a rubber of white polish. When the work is dry, cover the whole work with a dark brown wax, rubbing well into any mouldings or carvings. Allow the wax to harden off, then rub over the surface with fine steel wool and rub hard with a rag.

To produce the final finish, apply carnauba wax and beeswax, rubbing in well again to produce that hard finish. As for finishing oak timbers, apply rottenstone, wipe off the surplus and polish off. The work should now have a nice mellow tone with a satin gloss finish with the look of years of wear.

Restoring an old finish

As mentioned previously the natural colour of the furniture must be kept if the value of the antique piece is to be maintained. Too often you will see antique furniture which has been heavily re-polished or even completely stripped and re-

FIG 75   *A dirty polished surface requiring cleaning*

finished when a simple reviving of the original finish would have been quite adequate. What is normally required is the removal of years of dirt and grime which has accumulated over the period of use. There are numerous ways of achieving a well-restored finish.

Most antique furniture will have been finished in polish, spirit varnish, oil varnish, wax or oil, and once you have determined what finish is likely to be on the work, you can proceed to restore the surface. A light solvent test should help determine the finish. Use a rag dampened with methylated spirits and lightly rub over an area behind a chair leg or at the side of a cabinet just to soften the finish. If the surface has been polished the finish should soften eventually. If the finish is oil-based, you will produce only a dull effect on the surface. Oil or wax surfaces also produces a similar effect.

The next stage is to remove all the dirt and grime. To do this I use one or two different mixtures which are usually quite successful. The first method is to use a mixture of methylated spirits and linseed oil, mixed two parts of methylated spirits to one part linseed oil. Using a rag or grade 000 steel wool, rub over the polished surface to remove the dirt. You will cut through the dirt, eventually showing the cleaner colour of the old polish underneath. The aim is to clean off all the dirt until the colour shows up all over the work. This will take considerable time and effort, but will be well worth it when complete. Allow the work to dry out when clean and then lightly paper down with fine flour paper or lubrisil paper and apply one thin coat of polish. Wipe over with a rubber of polish after lightly papering the first coat. Now the work can be waxed with a soft beeswax or even a dulling matt wax, depending on the texture of finish required.

The second method of cleaning is by applying turpentine and linseed oil with 000 steel wool. This method is often good for oil-based varnishes, wax and oil finishes. The mixture does not penetrate too deeply in the surface and simply removes the dirt and grime by abrasion from the steel wool and lubrication from the turps and oil. Again, the surface will take on a dull appearance when cleaned and should be lightly papered down when dry. If sufficient protection is still there when cleaned, then all that is required is a good waxing down with a good quality wax to bring back the finish to a good, clean, bright, restored finish.

The third method is to use an abrasive such as pumice powder, applied with a damp rag. Rub over the surface to remove the dirt and grime making sure you don't cut through the old finish to the timber, otherwise you may change the colour of the patina and cause a patchy effect which is very difficult to restore. A mixture of turpentine and linseed oil can also be used as a lubricant for the pumice powder in place of water – usually you will find this produces a smoother cut. When the cutting back is finished clean off all the surplus pumice powder by wiping the work with turpentine or water. Allow the surface to dry out before the next stage. Lastly, restore the old finish with wax as in the previous methods, giving a good rub over to remove all the excess.

Revivers

When a polished surface loses its gloss and becomes dull a simple reviving of the surface is needed. A reviver cleans the surface and brings up the gloss by a simple abrasion of the polished surface.

An old traditional reviver was made by mixing butter of antimony, linseed oil, vinegar, methylated spirits and camphor. This mixture was applied to a polish surface with cotton wadding, rubbing in straight lines and circular motions until the surface was brought to a bright glossy finish. The work was then dusted over with a soft clean cloth or duster.

Generally, revivers are just a simple cleaning agent but can also incorporate abrasives which help to cut into the polished surface producing a burnishing effect. There is also what is commonly known as a 'haze' remover, which, when applied, helps to remove any final fine paste or wax which was used in the burnishing process. Sometimes a fine chalk can also be added to the reviver to help remove these pastes and waxes. The chalk changes the reviver into a fine cream. Nowadays revivers are produced in creams and emulsions and are quite good if used correctly. However, because some of them incorporate silicones, they can create finishing problems at a later stage.

I prefer to use a good quality cream rather than a wax because the cream cleans the surface with a fine cutting action, whereas a wax tends to leave a deposit which, no matter how thin, will hold a certain amount of dust. It is imperative that you use one reviver only; do not mix waxes and creams together on one surface. If you do this you will produce an accumulation of dirt and grime together with a dull surface.

On open grain timbers such as oak, teak or elm, however, use only wax-based materials. If you use white creams, sometimes a white or greyish deposit can be left behind in the pores of the grain; and if the colour of the timber is dark, then the cream will show up even more.

Finally, to be safe, it is probably better to use a cream reviver which, when rubbed over the polished surface becomes transparent on application, thus leaving the surface clean and bright. Always remove all the surplus cream, rubbing well with a clean rag and finish off with a soft clean duster. Remember, choose your revivers with care – don't always believe what it says on the label; if possible test them before purchase.

FIG 76 *Applying a mixture of turps and linseed oil to clean an old polished surface*

Chemicals

Common name	Supplier	Form	Uses
American potash	Chemists/ironmongers	Flakes or lumps	Weathering oak
Amonnia .880	Chemists/ironmongers	Liquid	Cleaning, adding to stain, fuming
Aniline dyes	Polish suppliers	Dry powders	Making stains and tinting polish
Bichromate of potash	Chemists/polish suppliers	Crystals or powder	For staining mahogany/oak
Burnt umber	Polish suppliers	Powder	Mixing in polishes for blinding out
Butter of antimony	Polish suppliers	Liquid	Used in some revivers
Camphorated oil	Chemists	Liquid	Revivers and removing heat marks
Caustic soda	Ironmonger/polish suppliers	Powder granules/flakes	Darkening oak, stripping finishes
China clay	Polish suppliers	Powder	Used in woodfillers
Chloride of lime	Chemists/polish suppliers	Powder	For weathering oak to a grey colour
Copal	Polish suppliers	Resin lumps	For making varnishes
Copperas, blue green	Chemists/polish suppliers	Blue or green crystals	For reducing the red in mahoganies
Driers (terebine)	Polish suppliers/paint suppliers	Yellow liquid	For speeding up the drying of paint or varnish
Gas black	Polish suppliers	Fine powder	Used for ebonizing
Gold size	Paint and polish suppliers	Gold liquid	For gilding, binding and fillers
Gum benzoin	Polish suppliers	Liquid	For making glaze
Hydrogen peroxide	Polish suppliers	Liquid	Used for bleaching timbers
Lime	Builders merchants	Powder or lumps	For liming oak and antique finishes
Linseed oil	Paint shops/polish suppliers	Liquid	Oil polishing and lubricating polish
Litharge	Polish suppliers	Powder	Used for colouring out
Methylated spirits	Polish suppliers/paint shops	Liquid	Used for making polishes and stains
Naphtha	Polish suppliers/paint shops	Yellow liquid	Making stains and some varnishes
Nitric acid	Chemists/polish suppliers	Clear liquid	Removing ink stains
Oxalic acid	Chemist/polish suppliers	Crystals	Light bleaching and removing marks
Plaster of Paris	Buildiers merchants/polish suppliers	Powder	For fillers on antique work
Precipitated chalk	Chemists/polish suppliers	Fine powder	Used as a substitute for Vienna chalk
Pumice powder	Chemists/polish suppliers	Graded grey powder	As an abrasive in French polishing
Rose pink	Polish suppliers	Powder	For making mahogany fillers
Rosin	Polish suppliers	Powder or lumps	Making stoppers, wax polishes
Rottenstone	Polish suppliers	Graded powder	For dulling down polish
Shellac	Polish suppliers	Various colours and grades	Making polish and stoppings
Silex	Polish suppliers	Powder	Making woodfillers
Soda	Chemists/ironmongers	Crystals	Removing dirt and grime off polish

Spirit colours
  Black
  Chrysoidine
  Green
  Mahogany
  Walnut
  Oak
  Yellow
  Pink
	Polish suppliers	Powders	For colouring polish and making stains for colouring timber

Sulphate of iron	Chemists/polish suppliers	Liquid	For ageing oak timbers
Sulphuric acid	Chemists	Liquid	Used in the acid finish

Chemicals used in finishing

The woodfinisher will in the course of his work be required to produce special colours and finishes. To achieve some of these finishes he will need to use certain chemicals. The list given below may help the reader become familiar with the names and uses of a selection of chemicals that could be of help in the course of his work.

Use of oil on antique furniture

Probably the easiest method of protecting timber is to use a simple oil finish, rubbed well into the timber surface. The ideal timbers for such oil finishes are teak, cedar and some walnuts. Various types of oil may be used to protect the timber but usually we use raw linseed oil or boiled linseed oil. Boiled linseed oil is usually a dark colour and has a slight darkening effect on the timber. Some oils can be dyed to produce richer colours. For example, a red oil can be used on some mahogany timbers to enhance the colour, and a walnut oil produces a darker effect on some walnut timbers, creating a deep rich colour and a dry dull texture.

Application of oil

The oil should be allowed to penetrate the timber surface and be rubbed well in with a clean rag. A good tip is to wipe over the surface to remove the excess oil and then lightly paper the surface while the oil is still wet, thus cutting into the timber. This will help to force the wet oil into the pores. Apply further coats about every 12 hours until a nice even coat is produced. When satisfied with the final appearance, rub the surface with a soft rag using plenty of pressure and work in short straight strokes. To produce a good sheen it may be necessary to apply quite a few coats to achieve the desired effect. The first application of oil will, of course, be absorbed by the timber. A well-oiled job should have a nice sheen to the surface, giving the timber a rich looking appearance. When working on large surfaces, for example large table tops, a wooden block with a felt pad fixed to the face is an ideal tool to use, to force the oil well into the timber surface. Constant friction with prolonged rubbing produces the smooth sheen required.

When restoring old furniture that has been

Chemicals

Common name	Supplier	Form	Uses
Tannic acid	Chemists	Powder	For fuming oak and adding colour
Toppings	Polish suppliers	Liquid	Used in polishing
Turpentine	Paint shops/polish suppliers	Liquid	Making waxes, stains, oil varnish
Vandyke brown	Polish suppliers	Powder	Mixed in polish for binding out
Vandyke crystals	Polish suppliers	Powder or crystals	Making water stains
Venetian red	Polish suppliers	Powders	Making mahogany filler and binding out
Vienna chalk	Polish suppliers	Powder	Used in the acid finish
Waxes			
Beeswax	Polish suppliers	Lumps or blocks	
Carnauba	Polish suppliers	Lumps	For making various graded wax polishes and stoppers
Japan	Polish suppliers	Soft lumps	
Paraffin	Polish suppliers	Blocks/lumps	
White spirit	Paint shops/polish suppliers	Liquid	Substitute for turps and making oil stains
Whiting	Builders merchants/polish suppliers	White powder	Making gesso and putty
Yellow ochre	Paint shops/polish suppliers	Powder	Making woodfillers and for blinding out
Zinc white	Paint shops/polish suppliers	Powder	Used in white liming oak and for blinding out

FIG 77 *Applying linseed oil on teak timber*

FIG 78 *Polishing off the surplus linseed oil with a clean rag*

oiled you need to remove dirt and grime before any re-oiling takes place. Wash down the furniture in turpentine with a very fine steel wool, grade 0000, or pumice powder to help abrade the surface. You should work carefully on the surface and try not to cut into the timber – otherwise you may produce light patches on the surface which may require re-colouring.

Re-oiling the work is done exactly as previously mentioned, but you must take care to clean off all the excess dirt and also make sure that the surface is clean and dry before hand. Allow at least 24 hours drying time before applying the oil. Make sure you do not remove any marks of character, including stains, ink marks or water marks. These marks must be left on the work so as to retain the value of the piece, especially if the furniture is a valuable antique.

Finally, the process previously referred to will require a great deal of time and effort; the pores of the timber are simply fed with oil, and no bodying up takes place as with French polishing. However, a short cut to the oil finish can be adopted. This finish can be classed as an oil-filled finish. The timber surface is simply filled with an oil-bound woodfiller as the first stage, and when dry the surface is papered down with fine paper and then coated with oil. Further coats may be needed depending on the type of finish required. The coloured oils can be used to add a little darkening, and if a certain texture is required, then fine steel wool can be used to produce a matt finish when the surface has dried out.

Waxing on antique furniture

A very simple and easy finish to produce which, when done correctly, will generally give good results. Unfortunately, wax does attract dirt and grime and is not highly resistant to normal domestic hazards. Wax produces a similar result to oils except there is more body in the final finish. It is used mainly on reproduction furniture, wall panelling and antiques.

Wax polishes are usually made from a basic mixture of beeswax and turpentine, yellow or white beeswax being dissolved in turpentine by heating in a bath of water until the wax is completely dissolved. Wax can be melted in cold turpentine but will take many hours to dissolve. Mix the wax sufficiently to provide a good consistency and therefore produce a creamy smooth paste.

FIG 79 *Waxing a mahogany chairframe using steelwool and wax (an alternative method of wax application)*

FIG 80 *Polishing off the surplus wax with a clean rag*

Application of wax

When the desired consistency has been achieved you can now apply the wax to the surface. Use a brush or rag and lay the wax over the surface evenly, avoiding any build up of surplus in corners or mouldings which could then dry hard and become difficult to remove. When you have covered the whole surface area, you should use a coarse rag to rub the wax in a circular motion well into the pores. The final finish can be produced by rubbing in the direction of the grain, using a soft clean rag. A good clean surface with a satin gloss should be the outcome of your efforts and after a few more hours, when the solvent has evaporated, you can further burnish the surface with the rag or a soft brush.

The beauty of a waxed finish is the ease with which it can be restored. The surface can always be revived by simple waxing providing all the dirt is removed before renovation takes place. Generally proprietary waxes are available from most polish suppliers in hard, medium and soft consistencies. A blend of hard wax can simply be made soft by adding a proportion of paraffin wax or if a much harder wax is required, then carnauba wax is normally added. This wax is somewhat difficult to melt owing to its high melting point but it is extremely hard.

When waxing light timbers, a bleached wax should be used to protect the natural colour. More often, however, a yellow wax is used and will prove quite satisfactory. Dry colours can also be added to waxes and some soluble dyes to tone up waxes for shading purposes. Some light transparent pigments may also be incorporated in the wax blend that in effect provide a wax type filler to enable the open grain to be filled if required.

If there are any discrepancies in the colour of the work, sometimes a thin film of polish can be applied before waxing, to help hold up the final finish and also make any necessary colour matching which may be required before the final wax finish.

Restoring the wax on antique furniture is similar to restoring the oil; all the dirt and grime must be removed. Work carefully, allow adequate drying after using the cleaning solvents and, above all, again leave any original marks, stains, etc. intact. A good waxed finish really looks effective and shows all the characteristics of the furniture – the aged look, the patina – and gives a quality appearance which can make a piece of furniture look really distinctive.

CHAPTER ELEVEN

Workshop practice

•

The subject of woodfinishing would not be complete without a thorough reference to the materials, tools and aids used in the workshop. Many materials are used in a polishing shop, and quite a few of the processes are dirty. Such processes can also produce waste, increase certain hazardous conditions, be unpleasant and above all produce dirty work. (See Chapter 1 on brushes and rags)

General layout
You should attempt to plan out the workshop so that it can accommodate almost any size of furniture. It should be situated with the windows facing northwards to give you a stable light for colouring purposes – overhead light, such as a skylight is the next best thing. Set out your benches so that you can easily work around them, preferably in the middle of the workshop. It is sensible to have a long bench against one wall with cupboards underneath and shelves above for storage. A sink providing washing facilities is a must, and you will also require some form of heating, especially in the winter months to help to provide a steady temperature when applying your finishes. It is very important to have a well-heated workshop otherwise the viscosity of the materials, especially polishes and varnishes, will be affected. A cold workshop may result in finishing problems related to some of the surface coatings.

Heating
The ideal system of heating a workshop would be to have a completely independent system, but obviously this would prove very expensive. Generally a good local heating system is all that is required. This could consist of slow running fan heaters with the flow directed in certain areas or as an alternative, convected heat which could be supplied by electricity. In one workshop I used to work in many years ago, infra-red heaters were used and proved very successful. Whatever system you decide to use in a polishing shop, you should endeavour to see that the system is safe and practical. No makeshift heating systems should be used or even thought of. Remember, some of the finishing materials that you will be using are flammable and could be highly dangerous in certain circumstances.

Workbenches
The polisher's workbench is similar to that of a joiner's bench, except there is no well or vice required. The bench can be made of timber frame with chipboard or a heavy plywood top. Alternatively, a metal framework with a solid wooden top can be used, giving more stability. Some of the older type benches were simply made of a flat top, probably tongue and grooved boarding and having a folding twin trestle-type base, the idea being that the trestles could be taken down, thus providing extra floor space for any larger work which might need finishing.

Abrasive papers
These materials are available in various forms from sheets to rolls and whatever type is purchased, they should be used with care and with

economy in mind. Abrasive papers are expensive and should be used in the correct manner and, in general, if used correctly, most will last quite a long time. Keep an old box at one side for old pieces of abrasive papers to be used on small work.

Solvents and thinners

Solvents and thinners are often overused and therefore become expensive commodities. If cleaning fluids are overused they will become less effective and useless for their particular purpose. When selecting a solvent for a particular job, use it sparingly and try to mix just enough material for the whole job in question.

One of the most common faults in using solvents is mixing too much colour when using spirit colours. Usually methylated spirits is the solvent which is overused here. A good method worth considering is to mix a range of spirit colours, full strength, and simply thin them down when required.

Pouring materials

Some wastage can be caused by bad pouring. With a variety of types of container it is not always easy to pour out the material without some wastage. Try to pour the material away from the lip nearest to the edge of the can, especially with cans containing methylated spirits, turpentine and linseed oil. Also always pour away from the can label, if at all possible, thus allowing any instructions on the label to be clearly seen and not obliterated in any way.

With such materials as strippers, be careful to pour them out carefully, and with the caustic type of stripper always cover with a rag and open with care because of the gaseous mixture.

Take care when handling any acid mixtures, bleaches and any other chemicals which may be a little hazardous. Read the labels carefully.

Containers

Any containers which require cleaning after use should be attended to immediately. If any

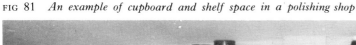

FIG 81 *An example of cupboard and shelf space in a polishing shop*

material is allowed to harden in a container, then it is most unlikely you will be able to clean it out. Do not leave small amounts of mixed materials lying around unmarked; it is uneconomical and usually only the original user will know what they are, how long they have been mixed, and what colours they were meant for. If any special colours are to be kept for a specific job, they should be put into a container and labelled correctly with the name of the colour and the type of material. Some containers can be boiled in a caustic soda solution, especially glass, ceramic and eathenware containers. For cleaning dye residues, sulphuric acid can be a useful cleaner, but use it with care.

Holding and supporting work

It is often difficult to work on certain jobs without having means of support for items such as small turned work, mouldings, laths, small carvings, fretwork and spindles. Having your bench set out as described previously, you will require a variety of holding devices and supports for some of the items mentioned. These devices could be any of

FIG 82 *Fixed trestles*

FIG 83 *Folding trestles*

the following:

Bench pads for supporting flat panel work, cabinet doors and long heavy mouldings or casement work.

Bench hooks or *tenter hooks* for holding short mouldings and small panel work.

Bench brackets for holding turned work and similar work in position.

Bench sticks or *battens* for holding small boxes or drawers whilst staining, filling or polishing.

Hand brackets are ideal for small pieces of work which are difficult to hold, one example being a wall bracket for shelving.

Support for carved work. Using a flat board, fix the backside of the carvings to the board by means of old newspapers and animal glue. Remove the carving by inserting an old knife or similar blade between the backside of the carving and the board. All the staining and polishing can be done whilst in the fixed position.

In conclusion, it is always better to pay some attention to designing some form of holding device for certain items of small work. Making good supports and holding devices will help you work comfortably and more efficiently. It is always worthwhile spending a little time on carefully thought out holding devices and supports.

Storing materials

Allow adequate storage in a workshop area; keep materials such as polish and varnish close at hand but lock up all dangerous chemicals.

Cleaning

Keep the workshop tidy and uncluttered. In my experience, the workshop was cleaned out once a week by the apprentices; the benches were swept clean, the shelves dusted off and the floors covered with wet sawdust and swept over until thoroughly clean. Remember that good work can only be done in a clean environment, and it is up to you to achieve this.

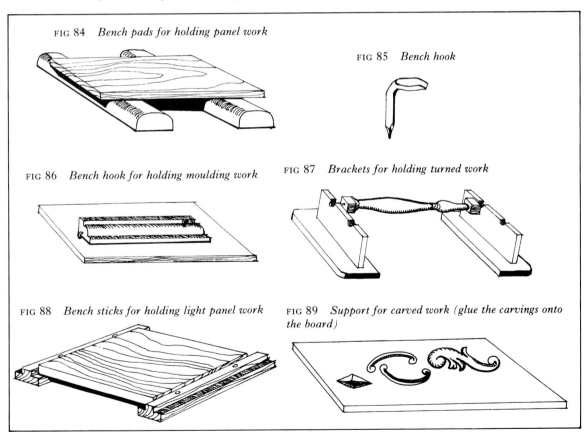

FIG 84   *Bench pads for holding panel work*

FIG 85   *Bench hook*

FIG 86   *Bench hook for holding moulding work*

FIG 87   *Brackets for holding turned work*

FIG 88   *Bench sticks for holding light panel work*

FIG 89   *Support for carved work (glue the carvings onto the board)*

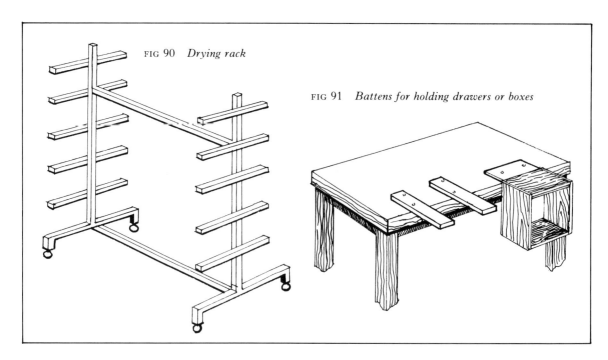

FIG 90 *Drying rack*

FIG 91 *Battens for holding drawers or boxes*

FIG 92 *Rack and storage systems in a polishing shop*

Storing work

The ideal situation is to have a room for storage purposes. Finished work and some work in progress could be stored well away from the main polishing workshop. This storage situation is something of a luxury but in the case of the old polishing shops of high class work was often the normality. Whilst work is in progress racking systems are a good thing to have. These racks are suitable for storing flat stock, such as panel work, small doors, loose table tops, and even small items such as clock cases and jewellery boxes.

Material stock control

Purchasing some materials can be difficult because of shelf life. For example, bleaches are unstable and should not be purchased in bulk, but only in small quantities as they lose strength over a period of time. Polishes and varnishes also have a shelf life and deteriorate. Woodfillers solidify if not used within a few months. Chemicals should be carefully checked from time to time in case of leakage. Some dyes and pigments can become damp if stored for any length of time and may

110

become unusable. Oil-based materials can oxidize and become hard and develop a skin such as linseed oil.

Avoid buying too much of one item, such as varnish, which polishers use less of than polish. A polisher would generally stock small quantities of the standard polish, but any special polishes such as red polish or black polish could be purchased for a specific job. The quantities to purchase would depend on work output but in general 5 l ($7\frac{1}{2}$ pt) containers are the largest size you should require.

Whatever liquid materials you purchase, always use the materials in sequence. Keep a good stock record and do not mix up your materials in storage, otherwise you may end up using new stock before old. This poor practice could lead to wastage in the long term, owing to deterioration of old stock.

One item which is usually not in store long enough for you to worry about is methylated spirits. This material tends to be used quite quickly, especially for thinning down polish, spirit varnish, mixing spirit dyes or for simply washing down after stripping off old polish.

An example of quantities of materials to be stored could be as follows:

25 l ($37\frac{1}{2}$ pt) button polish

10 l (15 pt) garnet polish
5 l ($7\frac{1}{2}$ pt) white polish
10 l (15 pts) transparent or special pale
25 l ($37\frac{1}{2}$ pt) methylated spirits
5 l ($7\frac{1}{2}$ pt) linseed oil
5 l ($7\frac{1}{2}$ pt) turps substitute
25 l ($37\frac{1}{2}$ pt) stripper
5 l ($7\frac{1}{2}$ pt) spirit varnish
5 l ($7\frac{1}{2}$ pt) polyurethane varnish
5 l ($7\frac{1}{2}$ pt) oak oil stain
5 l ($7\frac{1}{2}$ pt) mahogany oil stain
5 l ($7\frac{1}{2}$ pt) walnut oil stain

The above list is of course just a guide; if you are just working with materials as a hobby, scale down the quantities to one fifth.

Any powder materials, dyes, pigments and such items as bleach, acids, abrasive papers and brushes should be purchased in small quantities. These materials are not used too often, so bulk purchase is not advisable. One point worth remembering though is abrasive papers are expensive and to purchase a large stock, if used quite often, could be a great cash saving. Finally, any woodfillers should be purchased when required. Remember, they do tend to go hard with time. Buy one tin of each colour – oak, walnut and mahogany.

CHAPTER TWELVE

Safety in woodfinishing

•

In general, most people in industry are becoming familiar with the *Health and Safety at Work Act 1974*. This act was largely founded on the principal recommendations of the Robins report on *Safety and Health at Work* published in 1972. However, the current act contains some significant aspects which did not appear in the previous recommendations.

General aims of the act

The main purposes of the act are to provide for the comprehensive and integrated system of law dealing with the health, safety and welfare of work people and also the health and safety of the public who may be affected by certain work activities. The act aims to change many people's attitudes towards health and safety and also the way in which the scope of heath and safety are administered. Many people who have never before been obliged to come within the scope of legislation will now be included. The most significant factor in relation to the act is the concern of the self-employed person, who previously was never obliged to even consider such an act. The act does not attempt to cover every situation or even to attempt to determine rules which could fit each and every working situation. The idea of the act is to attempt to make certain concepts applicable to the working people at large.

When the act came into force on the 1st April 1975, the employer was made responsible for employees with regard to their safety and health and for ensuring that the public were not harmed by his employees' work activities. The legislation does include an innovation which could be introduced by any future regulations – namely, that if any employer intends to carry out certain work which is dangerous or even a threat to health, if something goes wrong he may be obliged to inform not only his employees but also the local population.

Application of the act

The new act applies to people in a working capacity: employers, self-employed, employees and certain members of the public. The new legislation largely replaces most of the old law on *Safety and Health in Industry*. Whilst we are mostly concerned with materials related to the woodfinishing trade, the act replaces the *Cellulose Regulations Act 1934* which was once part of the *Factory and Workshop Act 1901*.

New legislation

The general principles of legislation apply wherever people work and the general principles may be set out as follows:

(*1*) The employer should ensure, so far as is reasonably practicable, the health, safety and welfare at work of all his employees. Therefore, he must maintain as far as is reasonably practicable, his plant and equipment, systems of work, so as to be safe and without risk to health.

(*2*) He must also ensure, so far as is reasonably practicable, that in using, handling, storing or transporting articles and substances there is no risk to health and safety.

(*3*) He must also provide relevant information, instructions, training and supervision as are necessary to ensure the health and safety of his employees.

(*4*) Places of work under the employer's control must be maintained in a condition that is safe and without risks to health and provide means of access to and egress from it that are safe and without risks.

(*5*) The working environment must be well maintained and, so far as is reasonably practicable, be safe without any risks to health, with regard to facilities and arrangements for general welfare at work.

The employer must prepare a written statement of his general policy with respect to health and safety of his employees and the organization and arrangements for carrying out that policy.

Where appropriate, after regulations have been made, employers can allow employees to set up their own safety representatives. This does not apply to self-employed persons who, of course, are responsible for their own acts and omissions, and at the same time are responsible for the health and safety of any other person (not in his employment) who may be at risk.

Enforcement

Local authorities are now responsible for the enforcement of the regulations under section 18 of the *Health and Safety at Work Act*. The local authorities are under guidance from the Health and Safety Executive. The authority appoints a local inspector giving him powers to act accordingly. Some of the powers which an inspector may invoke are to:

(*a*) Enter a premises to carry out his effective duty.

(*b*) Take with him a constable to apprehend any person obstructing him in the execution of his duty.

(*c*) Take with him any other person he may require in the execution of his duty.

(*d*) Take any necessary photographs or measurements of the premises.

(*e*) Take samples or any articles he may require.

(*f*) Take any books or documents which may be relevant.

(*g*) Require any person to provide assistance in any matter relating to the execution of his powers.

The Highly Flammable Liquids and Liquefied Petroleum Gases Regulations 1972

The above regulations came into operation in June 1973 and the *Cellulose Regulations* were revoked.

The new regulations are concerned with the following materials:

Material	Definition
(*1*) Aqueous ammonia	Ammonia gas dissolved in water
(*2*) Commercial butane	A hydrocarbon mixture which may consist of butane or butylene
(*3*) Commercial propane	A hydrocarbon mixture which may consist of propane or propylene
(*4*) Dangerous vapours	A concentration of vapours greater than the lower flammable limit of the vapour
(*5*) Highly flammable liquids	Any liquid which gives off a flammable vapour at a temperature of less than 32° celsius when ignited.

Storage

Storerooms and containers should be provided and marked accordingly. Every bin, tank or vessel used for storing a highly flammable liquid should be marked as highly flammable or flashpoint below 32°C or flashpoint in the range of 22°C to 32°C.

Labelling of dangerous substances

All containers and packages should be marked and are classified under either one or two of the following categories:

(*1*) as explosive, oxidizing, highly flammable or flammable

FIG 93 *Key to symbols for labelling products*

KEY TO SYMBOLS

 HIGHLY FLAMMABLE
FLASH POINT
BELOW 21°C

 PRODUCTS WITH
FLASH POINT IN THE
RANGE 21°C-55°C
CARRY NO SYMBOL
BUT SHOW THE
DESIGNATION
FLAMMABLE

 PRODUCT
CLASSIFIED AS
HARMFUL

 PRODUCT
CLASSIFIED AS
CORROSIVE

 PRODUCT
CLASSIFIED AS
IRRITANT

NO SYMBOL WILL BE USED
IF THE PRODUCT IS NOT
CLASSIFIED

THE LAYOUT MAY VARY
FROM THIS EXAMPLE BUT
THE INFORMATION WILL BE
PRESENTED SUBSTANTIALLY
AS SHOWN.

(2) as toxic, corrosive, harmful or irritant

The regulations were passed in September 1984 and came into effect in January 1986 in order to bring about a standard of labelling within the EEC. This standardisation will help to avoid any possible misunderstandings which could arise from the existence of different regulations within each country, especially when goods are transported across national frontiers.

Information which must be specified in detail must be shown on the label. The new labels will show commercial information such as description, reference and batch numbers and, in a separate section of the label, symbols and phrases which apply to the particular material.

Flammability – will be indicated by a flame symbol with the words highly flammable if the flash point is below 21°C or by the word flammable without the symbol if the flash point is between 21°C and 55°C.

Health hazards – will be indicated by a named symbol when the material is harmful or corrosive or irritant.

Certain constituents – will be nominated if their concentration exceeds a specified level in a product classified overall as harmful, corrosive or irritant.

Petroleum mixtures – can be identified by the words petroleum mixture giving off a flammable heavy vapour not to be exposed near a flame, printed in the commercial section of the label. Note that the red diamond will no longer be displayed. Although one section of the label will be reserved for information required by these regulations, the commercial section of the label will continue to show details required by other regulations relating to: Petroleum mixtures (as already described); the presence of isocyanates;

FIG 94 *Tin of barrier cream*

and the presence of lead.

Whilst the composition of some materials will remain unchanged, some new labels which, together with all other suppliers of materials to be brought into use, may give rise to some queries. Explanation and some guidance will be available through your material supplier and should be sought immediately if in any doubt.

Fire and Explosion

All surface coatings other than the water-borne materials have a fire risk. This risk applies both to the storage and use of these coatings. In general there is a division between some materials which are put into two categories 'low flash' and 'high flash'. When dealing with fire and explosion we are concerned with three main areas, these being flammability, inflammability and combustion.

(1) *Flammability* – Gases which can be ignited by flame together with liquids and solids whose vapours can be so ignited. Example: acetone.

(2) *Inflammability* – Substances which can be ignited without flame and certain chemical reactions producing heat. Example: contaminated rags.

(3) *Combustion* – Liquids and solids which will burn on the application of a flame. Examples: oils, resins.

Obviously there are national regulations which can be interpreted by the local authority who in some special cases may enforce an additional bye-law. Some of these bye-laws could include the siting of a building, fire exits, extraction of fumes, disposal of waste products and the storage of flammable liquids.

Adequate insurance cover should be taken out to provide comprehensive cover of all risks related to fire, accident, damage to property and equipment.

Hazards

Some of the materials used in the finishing shop may be toxic and give off toxic vapours. One material used in strippers is methylene chloride and this can be very powerful, so necessary precautions must be taken regarding adequate ventilation.

Polyurethane materials are a particular danger owing to their isocyanate content, which is highly toxic. There are strict regulations governing the use of such materials which must be strictly adhered to.

Dust

Most materials used in the furniture industry produce some kind of dust. The inhalation of dust can be harmful. You may use dust extractors and, of course, masks. Usually dust is caused by the sanding of timber or surface coatings.

Skin irritation

The skin contains oils and fats in the glands and should not be dried up in any way. Any prolonged wetting of the hands with solvents may eventually cause dermatitis. The skin can be aggravated even further if the person is in poor health. Sometimes a French polisher's skin can become irritated by using solvents such as methylated spirits or turpentine substitute. The irritation may take the

FIG 95 *Fire extinguishers, CO_2, dry powder*

FIG 96   *First-aid box*

form of dermatitis (inflammation often caused by flaking or fissuring). The use of patent barrier creams helps to combat dermatitis if used regularly. Some soap materials containing sulphur can also help.

Inhalation

Problems are caused through inhaling gases, vapours of volatile liquids and solids to particles in the form of mists, or droplets and solid particles in dusts. Inhalation of the above can cause a depressant action and affect you like anaesthetic.

Acid burns

The woodfinisher may handle many chemicals in the course of his work and the hazards are usually minor ones. Some problems may arise in using hydrochloric acid, sulphuric acid or nitric acid. When using these acids always protect the skin. Any mixing of acids with water should be done with care. Always add the acid to the water. Any splashing of acid on the skin should be dealt with immediately. Wash the acid off with water.

Alkali burns

One strong alkali often used by the woodfinisher is caustic soda. Handle this material with care and always *half* fill any container with this material because of its foaming capacity when added to water. Any contact with the skin should be dealt with immediately. Wash with water, dry off and apply a smooth skin cream.

Any large areas of skin which receive acid burns should receive treatment at hospital immediately. Always protect the eyes when using these materials and again wash the eyes with water if they become contaminated. If severe burns result from using acids or alkalis you must seek hospital treatment.

Bibliography

1 Collier, J. W. and Dixon, G. *Mending and Restoring Furniture* Garnstone Press Ltd, London 1972.
2 Collier, J. W. *Woodfinishing* Pergamon Press, Oxford 1967.
3 Hayward, C. H. *Staining and Polishing* Evans Bros, London 1975; Drake, New York 1975.
4 Oil and Colour Chemists Association. *Solvents, Oils, Resins and Driers* Chapman and Hall, London 1961.
5 H.M.S.O. *Health and Safety at Work Act 1974.*
6 Parry, J. P. *Graining and Marbling* Crosby Lockwood and Son Ltd, London 1949.

Index